T0293628

ROUTLEDGE LIBRARY EDITIONS:
MANAGEMENT

Volume 41

MANAGEMENT AND SOCIETY IN SWEDEN

MANAGEMENT AND SOCIETY IN SWEDEN

PETER LAWRENCE AND TONY SPYBEY

Routledge
Taylor & Francis Group

LONDON AND NEW YORK

First published in 1986 by Routledge & Kegan Paul plc

This edition first published in 2018
by Routledge
2 Park Square, Milton Park, Abingdon, Oxon OX14 4RN

and by Routledge
711 Third Avenue, New York, NY 10017

Routledge is an imprint of the Taylor & Francis Group, an informa business

British Library Cataloguing in Publication Data
A catalogue record for this book is available from the British Library

ISBN: 978-1-138-55938-7 (Set)
ISBN: 978-1-351-05538-3 (Set) (ebk)
ISBN: 978-1-138-57304-8 (Volume 41) (hbk)
ISBN: 978-0-203-70168-3 (Volume 41) (ebk)

Publisher's Note
The publisher has gone to great lengths to ensure the quality of this reprint but points out that some imperfections in the original copies may be apparent.

Disclaimer
The publisher has made every effort to trace copyright holders and would welcome correspondence from those they have been unable to trace.

MANAGEMENT AND SOCIETY IN SWEDEN

Peter Lawrence
and
Tony Spybey

ROUTLEDGE & KEGAN PAUL
LONDON

First published in 1986 by
Routledge & Kegan Paul plc
11 New Fetter Lane, London EC4P 4EE

Set in 10/12 pt Sabon Linotron 202
by Inforum Ltd, Portsmouth
and printed in Great Britain
by Billing & Sons Ltd, Worcester

British Library Cataloguing in Publication Data

Lawrence, P.A. (Peter Anthony) 1937–
    Management and society of Sweden.
    1. Industrial management——Sweden
    I. Title II. Spybey, Tony
    658'.009485   HD70.S/

ISBN 0–7102–0686–0

To Runo and Anki,
and to Victoria

Contents

Since this book was written a tragic and uncharacteristically Swedish event has taken place in Stockholm, the assassination of prime minister Olof Palme. This represents a sad loss to the text of this book as well as the more significant one to the Swedish people, more devastating than outsiders can imagine, and to the world as a whole.

Acknowledgments

Tony Spybey would particularly like to thank his friends Runo Axelson of the University of Uppsala and David Wilson of the University of Warwick for the help they have given.

Peter Lawrence would like to thank the Economic and Social Research Council for a grant enabling him to visit Sweden and study Swedish management at first hand, and the Department of Industrial Economics and Management at the Royal Institute of Technology in Stockholm for their hospitality during the period of this visit. He would also like to thank the many managers he interviewed and companies he visited in Sweden for their interest and hospitality. Finally he is aware of having benefited a great deal from discussions with various officials, with the Swedish Employers' Federation, with the Engineering Association, with the Central Statistical Office, with a number of consultants, head-hunters, and business journalists, and with a range of academics and teachers at the Swedish Management Group, Stockholm University, Uppsala University and the Royal Institute of Technology.

The authors alone were responsible for any errors and for the interpretation.

1 Past and present

Two things seem to characterise Swedish history. One is the lateness of arrival of certain pervasive influences, particularly religion and industrialisation; the other is the way in which the social structure has evolved in a simple and straightforward form. Examples of the latter are the consistently centralised élite and the homogeneity of language, culture and religion. In Britain, in contrast, there is the feeling that being the first on a number of occasions has left untidy structures, physical and social, which make the society difficult to govern and, especially, to change.

Religion came to Sweden as late as the ninth century and then took some three centuries to become really established. Paganism still existed in the sixteenth century at the time, 1544, that the Catholic Church was replaced by Lutheranism. The sixteenth century is generally recognised as the time of the foundation of the Swedish national state, when King Gustav Vasa established independence in an age of greatness, when Sweden held sway over Finland, Denmark and parts of Germany, Austria and Poland. By the seventeenth century there was, in addition, a putative 'New Sweden' on land bought from the indians, by the Delaware River in North America, as well as holdings on the west coast of Africa, allowing for participation in the slave trade. Vasa's name is commemorated in the warship of the time recovered from the sea off Stockholm and restored on the waterfront there in a much more complete form than the comparable *Mary Rose* in England.

Today, many people see Sweden's oft-projected role as the 'world's conscience' as symptomatic of its reluctance to accept small-state status. Swedes like to see their statesmen taking part in world affairs for peace and compromise, and Olof Palme, the Social Democratic Labour leader, currently represents the epitome of this.

Since the establishment of the Lutheran church, Swedes have traditionally all been members of a single state church and have in fact elected their clergy. By the seventeenth century church and state had become one, and from that structure emerged the universities as,

almost exclusively, institutions of preparation for government service, a prerogative of the higher echelons of society. The state
bureaucrats, the clergy and the university teachers were all civil
servants, and until the twentieth century this was the mechanism for
the centralisation of the Swedish élite which consistently filled all
important government posts. Today church attendance is at a level
of 3.3 per cent, which is even lower than Britain and, of course, much
lower than America (Tomasson, 1970). The structure of the élite is
now different, however, as will be seen from the ensuing text, yet
attempts by recent governments to disestablish the church have
always been thwarted and it remains a vestigial link with the past.

One legacy of the Swedish state church is that there is no religious
divide for anyone to make a focal point of, and religion thus tends to
represent the past, whereas Sweden is a forward-looking country. As
Tomasson (1970, p. 4), points out, Sweden's development as a
'homogeneous society lacking the cleavages of many others' has left
it with relatively straightforward class and city–country divisions,
whilst the dominant value system that has developed more recently is
one of 'social reformism'. Where social cleavages did arise were
chiefly in the industrialisation process, particularly amongst the
Norrland saw-mills. These developments are well recorded in the
many industrial museums that Swedish communities maintain in
order to understand their past; in political terms they explain the
early radicalisation of the working class that led to the foundation of
the *Socialdemokratiska Arbetarepartiet* (literally Social Democratic
Labour Party – SAP for short) and the trades union movement. But
against all this the rationality and practicality of a Lutheran background comes through in the present-day Swede.

As part of its initial backwardness, Sweden missed out on the
feudal system and the economic structure that went with it. The
peasants were never suppressed to the degree that they were in the
rest of Europe, and to a large part were owners, under the Crown, of
their own land (Tomasson, 1970). On this basis they were consistently represented in the parliaments called by the King. It is difficult
to avoid the impression that this was a solid foundation for the high
level of involvement in and enthusiasm for government, engendering
an ingrained respect for the law for which Sweden has become so
renowned.

As Koblik (1975) points out, in the late eighteenth century 75 per
cent to 80 per cent of the Swedish population worked in agriculture.
By the late nineteenth century the figure was still as high as 72 per
cent, even though, meanwhile, an agricultural revolution had taken

place led by one Rutger Maclean and using many ideas from Britain, particularly those of Robert Bakewell, 'Turnip' Townsend and Jethro Tull. The government sponsored an enclosure movement, including land distribution and the exploitation of newly-reclaimed land, for which capital was apparently available in the rural areas. The population increased as a result of a series of bumper harvests and the introduction of the potato, and the numbers of independent farmers increased, followed, as the nineteenth century wore on, by a similar increase in the numbers of landless rural labourers, as Table 1.1 shows.

Table 1.1 **Independent farmers and landless labourers (1775–1870)**

Year	Independent Farmers	Landless Labourers
1775	1,052,725	548,827
1800	1,102,120	735,427
1870	1,395,543	1,288,206

(Koblik, 1975)

These features are reminiscent of the familiar pathway from agrarian society to industrial society, yet the pattern and sequence is very different from the British prototype. More than anything else, the Swedes today have been left with strong connections with the countryside: their gardens have no fences and ideally back on to the forest; many have been able to keep their family farm-houses as second homes, ideally in the far north.

When modernisation came to Sweden it came rapidly. The transition from agrarian to industrial society took place between 1890 and 1920. For various reasons it did not produce the problematic city sprawls to anything like the extent of other industrial revolutions, and Sweden has emerged from the process with a remarkably high proportion of its population living outside the main urban centres. Even today there are only three cities of any size:

Stockholm	1,300,000 inhabitants
Gothenburg	700,000 inhabitants
Malmö	500,000 inhabitants

What the rapid change did bring, however, was liberalism, socialism, parliamentarianism, industrialism and popular democracy (Tomasson, 1970). A link between the past and the future of this rapid industrialisation was the fact that the middle-class never leapt ahead of the working-class in terms of consumption (Himmelstrand and Lindhagen, 1976, pp. 227–8). In the past there had been no feudalism, the peasants had never been as oppressed as they had in most of Europe; in the future the high standard of living would be available to the middle-class and the working-class alike, enabling them both to develop a great belief in Swedish progress and even connect this with SAP politics. First, however, it may be helpful to consider an early episode of parliamentarianism during the so-called 'age of freedom'.

The age of freedom 1718–72

In the mid-eighteenth century Swedish society was made up, according to Carlsson (1975), roughly as follows:

0.5% population	Nobility	the four estates
1.0% population	Clerics	represented in
2.0% population	Burghers	the Riksdag
50.0% population	Peasants	
40+% population	Unpropertied, disenfranchised	

There was a well-developed parliamentary system, guaranteeing the representation of the four estates as listed above, and it came into its own during this period. The two parliamentary groups, not political parties outside of the *Riksdag*, were referred to as the 'Hats' and the 'Caps'. The former were named after the dashing tricorn hat, and stood for vigorous mercantilism and alliance with the French; the latter were named after old ladies' nightcaps, and were seen as timid. After a dominant early period on the part of the Hats, the two exchanged power a number of times up to the end of the period. The Hats represented the aristocratic state office-holders and, significantly, the mercantilist entrepreneurs in the already-developed iron industry, plus some peasants who were, after all, independent landowners on a small scale in their own right, whilst the Caps, especially the Younger Caps, pursued Whiggish liberal politics.

Closer examination of the period, however, reveals that this early parliamentary democracy, involving even the peasantry, was not without its limitations. Perhaps not surprisingly, these limitations were effected by the aristocracy through their grasp of the mechanisms of the state. Right up to the twentieth century the tradition survived in Sweden of bureaucrats, of noble birth, usually trained at the universities, who enjoyed the royal assent and the prerogative of

state office. In the parliamentary system just described, they operated through the ominously-named Secret Committee, which consisted of fifty nobles, twenty-five clergy and twenty-five burghers,
but no peasants. They controlled the spending of public finance; the
people had the right to decide their own taxation through parliament
but the Secret Committee decided how to spend it. The Secret
Committee also controlled foreign policy, which, incidentally, involved friendliness to France and enmity to Russia, long a Swedish
tradition. An important effect of this was that control of the *Riksdag*
depended on getting the support of the aristocrats, thus in effect
severely limiting parliamentarianism.

Three-quarters of the way through the eighteenth century, however, the King, Gustav III, became tired of the antics of parliament
and nobles alike. He intervened in a bloodless coup in 1772 and by
1789 had re-established royal absolutism, with a constitution
guaranteeing his own personal power. This ushered in the Gustavian
period which lasted up to the establishment of the present Swedish
constitution in 1809. The Gustavian age was noted for the establishment of the Swedish Academy, separate academies for music and art
and the development of theatre and literature.

Nineteenth-century Swedish history

In the first decade of the nineteenth century Sweden's alliance with
France brought defeat and the abdication and flight of King Gustav
Adolph. This led to the 1809 constitution, which owes something to
Montesquieu, the French radical liberal, as indeed did the outcome
of the events in France at that time as well as the American
constitution (the Swedish constitution is the second-oldest written
constitution after the latter). Stjernquist (1975, pp. 39–40) describes
it as seeking a middle road between the *Riksdag* politics of the 'age of
freedom' and the absolutism of Gustav III. The King retained two
votes in the highest executive, which consisted of four secretaries of
state and a cabinet containing a minister of justice, a foreign minister
and a court chancellor, plus six other ministers in an advisory
capacity. With the King in such a prominent position it was debated
ever afterwards which came first, the King or the constitution.
However, the historical sequence was that the *Riksdag* first established the constitution and then elected a King who was invited to
take office. Curiously to the outsider, it was one of Napoleon's
marshalls, Jean Bernadotte, who was chosen to become Karl I Johan

and to establish the royal dynasty which remains to this day. Such are the vicissitudes of history.

As explained already, all sections of Swedish society, with the exception of landless labourers, had been represented in the *Riksdag* for some time. Now the King's decisions were supposed to be voluntarily agreed to by all the four estates, the deliberations of the peasants' representatives being made away from the royal presence so that they would not be over-awed. Significantly, to all of this democratic provision was added both a free press law and, to handle public grievances, the role of Ombudsman, so widely linked ever since with Scandinavian procedures. However, the grasp of the aristocratic élite over the senior government posts remained and, although there was no organised conservative party, these state bureaucrats were conservative by nature and inclination and usually were loyal to the King who, in turn, saw them as chosen advisers. When party politics proper came at the beginning of the twentieth century it was thus against the background of a traditional conservative hegemony.

Of special interest for any comparison with other countries is the fact that the constitution provides for government decisions to be documented and for the documents to be publicly available. This applies to the appointment of government officials, including teachers and clergymen. This is the very reverse of policy in Britain, yet it is considered essential by the Swedes and to repeal the Act of Constitution would require two Acts of Parliament, with a general election taking place in between them.

After the ensovereignment of Jean Bernadotte, in 1812 Sweden joined the allies to fight Napoleon and, as a consequence, lost its sway over Finland to Russia, its long-term adversary. In return it gained Norway from Denmark, but the union was never a success, based as it was on geography rather than culture, communications and economic ties. The only notable outcome was the emigration of some Swedish workers to Norway, the 'grey' or 'raw' Swedes, some of whom were to build the famous railway line from Kiruna to Narvik for one of Sweden's export routes for iron.

Social change

Mass education was achieved in Sweden by 1842 and its introduction was more directed and enacted than in Britain, which probably accounts for the fact that it preceded the British pathway which, by evolutionary methods, did not achieve the same thing until 1871.

Despite this early progress, divisions remained in the system for quite a long time. Girls were not admitted to state gymnasia, the equivalent of English grammar schools, until 1926 and separate intellectual and practical forms of school eduction survived until the 1940s. This is probably due to the fact that initially the SAP, reformist in its entry to power between the turn of the century and 1932, did not make educational reform a priority, preferring to concentrate on economic and political matters. Conversion to comprehensive schools did not come until the 1960s, as in the UK. Unlike the UK, however, there was relatively little opposition and when the conversion came it was as a full-scale change-over to comprehensives, more centralised and more accepted, not partial or piece-meal (Tomasson, 1970; Härnquist and Bengtsson 1976).

Perhaps more striking and of more relevance to any industrial analysis were the advances in higher education. The 'Oxbridge' of Sweden, the universities of Uppsala and Lund, had existed since the fifteenth century in the case of Uppsala and the seventeenth century in the case of Lund, although previously the latter had been a Danish university when the Danes occupied that part of southern Sweden. However when higher education was extended it was mainly in the direction of *Tekniska Högskolar* (technical universities), after 1877, there being only five universities until the 1960s (Tomasson, 1970). This development was along the lines of the German model, with technology being highly regarded and introduced at the highest level of education before the end of the nineteenth century. It was quite the opposite in Britain where, despite the pioneering work both of the Faculty of Engineering at the University of Cambridge and of Imperial College in the University of London, technological education at that level was much in the minority until well after the Second World War. In fact, the up-grading of the colleges of advanced technology to universities in 1966 was the first extensive sign of a change of policy. Today 73 per cent of graduates in Sweden are in the technical field, as compared with 60 per cent in the rest of Europe, Britain being below the European average.

Economic growth

According to Jörberg (1975), economic growth in Sweden accelerated in three short periods during the nineteenth century. However, although this growth was export-led, as all Swedish growth has been, it was at first due to agriculture rather than industry. During the 1850s the first period of acceleration was when the export of grain assumed impressive proportions. Much of it was in the form of oats exported to London to help feed the army of some 300,000 horses that were required to keep the omnibuses running! In 1800, despite the fact that 80 per cent of the population worked on the land, as indeed they did throughout the nineteenth century, Sweden was not able to feed itself. By the 1850s, however, it was feeding a rapidly increasing population:

1800	2,300,000	
1860	3,900,000	
1900	5,200,000	(despite large-scale emigration)
		(Jorberg, 1975)

and producing a substantial surplus. The land reforms mentioned earlier in this chapter had certainly produced dividends.

It was during the 1870s that the second period of acceleration, which was an industrial one, began to have an effect on the economy. Iron ore had been produced and exported for a long time, but between 1830 and 1860 the production of iron itself increased substantially. During the same period timber production moved from the inland water-driven sites to steam-powered mills on the Baltic coast, allowing for easy shipment and export, while at the same time that archetypal industry, cotton, increased its production in Sweden twenty-fold, responding to demand, and the industrial workforce swelled proportionately (Jörberg, 1975). The rise in national income now became attributable to productivity and not just to population increase. Investments reached new heights and there was a railway boom, sorely needed to transport the exports to the ports of the Baltic and the Norwegian coast. And so Sweden's industrial revolution proceeded.

The third period of acceleration, during the 1890s, was due to the increase in home demand. Even by 1870 the equality between consumption and production had made Sweden an exception to the general rule for industrialising nations. Agriculture and industry had both been export-led, exports providing the broad market needed for scale and efficiency, whilst the development of saw-mills and iron-works generated the capital-goods production which has served Sweden so well ever since. The government invested heavily in education and communication, and private entrepreneurs emerged from the old merchant houses of Sweden, with their foreign connections helpful for foreign investment, a factor dating back to when Sweden was a great maritime power (Jörberg, 1975).

In 1868 and 1869, however, there were two consecutive bad

harvests which precipitated large-scale Swedish emigration to the United States. Initially 70,000 people left at one fell swoop, these not being the poorest, who were too poor to extract themselves (Akerman, 1975). There also took place a movement of landless labourers into the towns, although it has to be said that this process was never so pronounced as it was in some other countries, nor were the towns created so large and sprawling. Swedish industry has avoided giant concentrations which have given rise to such misery in other countries (Samuelsson, 1975). However the combined consequences of the two types of migration were felt most in the countryside. In 1870 75 per cent of the Swedish population worked in agriculture but by 1900 the proportion was reduced to 55 per cent – still, of course, high by British standards. After 1920 Sweden became primarily a country of immigration, chiefly from Finland but later supplemented by an influx of labour from Turkey, Yugoslavia and to some extent Asia.

Between 1872 and 1910 'much of what happened in Sweden echoed what had happened in Germany a few years earlier' (Tomasson, 1970). This trend embraced education, politics and intellectual life, replacing the previous French influence and in turn being replaced by British and American influences.

Twentieth-century Swedish history

Until the early twentieth century, then, Sweden was behind the rest of Europe, including Denmark and Norway, but it caught up fast. Furthermore it did so with an absence of severe argument, although the period between 1906 and 1914 was one of considerable turmoil.

The year 1905 was marked by the end of the union with Norway, which had never been a success, and the emergence of the first real party-government in Sweden, when the *Folkpartiet* (Liberal Party) briefly came to power. Between 1905 and 1914 the three great battles fought on the home front were the suffrage issue, the General Strike and the defence issue (Schiller, 1975). In the process of this the 'Liberals' unity was broken and the Left suffered setbacks. Schiller (1975) refers to these years as the 'years of crisis'. Essentially it was a struggle between left- and right-wing tendencies in politics, against a background of increasing industrialisation. The saw-mills were being transformed into pulp-mills in order to produce more of a finished product and a higher return on capital. Swedish engineering was beginning to produce the ball-bearings, telephones, separators and turbines for which it was to become famous. Domestic industry was turning to ready-made clothing and shoes for a more affluent population with more sophisticated tastes. In the process increased union membership was adding strength to the Federation of Labour Unions, the *Landsorganisationen i Sverige* (LO for short) which had been founded in 1898 by the SAP, itself founded in 1889. The concentration of industrial ownership was doing the same thing for the Employers' Association, *Svenska Arbetsgivareföreningen* (SAF), which had emerged in 1902.

The 1905 *Folkpartiet* (Liberal) government under prime minister Staaf was the first pure party-government, replacing the long domination of élite government ministers as advisers to the King. The latter were conservative by nature and inclination, but they did not constitute a conservative party, organised along the lines that we would recognise, until the General Voters' Alliance, the forerunner of the modern Moderate Alliance (Conservative) Party, emerged in 1904 (Elder, 1970, p. 3). The *Riksdag*, since the Great Reform of 1866, had consisted of a first chamber, the Upper House, the preserve of the landed gentry and big business; and a second chamber, the Lower House, the preserve of the middle class, both urban and rural. The former was elected through twenty-four provincial councils, the latter being elected directly, although suffrage was only available to 7 per cent of the population.

The chief aim of the Liberals was to push through provisions for universal suffrage because this would end the traditional Conservative hegemony. The Conservatives opposed it because it would make the lower chamber more important, which was quite true. The stumbling block continued to be the partnership between the King and the Conservatives. The King appeared to align himself with the Conservatives' opposition to suffrage and in doing so made the Liberals appear to be against the King. It was thus a struggle between popular and upper-class rule and when the suffrage gambit failed the Liberal government resigned.

There followed a coalition of conservatives and moderates, including the farmers, who had not yet formed a political party. These, too, had proposals for parliamentary reform, including the proportional representation for the Lower House that was to be brought in in 1910, but it was all in a form that would ensure a sizeable Conservative majority.

On the industrial relations front, against the background of a rapidly-consolidating industrial society, 1906 saw the employers association, SAF, accepting collective bargaining in principle. By 1907, however, they were demanding the maintenance of the freedom to hire and fire, which led to what is considered a milestone in Swedish labour history, the 'December compromise', confirming the right of unions to organise labour in return for the SAF's demand. This is still a fundamental principle of industrial relations in Sweden.

However this still did not satisfy everybody. The shipyard workers challenged the employer's right to hire and fire in 1908 and it led to some very ugly incidents, including the use of English strike-breakers and a retaliatory bomb outrage, the Almathea incident, usually attributed to the Young Socialists, an extreme left wing of the Social Democrats. This group were trying to urge the SAP, against the better judgment of their leader Hjalmar Branting, into more revolutionary tactics. Equally against Branting's better judgment, as well as that of the LO leadership, the continuing strikes and lock-outs took the country to the verge of a general strike. Branting felt, quite correctly, that such a strike would prejudice the suffrage issue by alienating the middle class, and in the event the LO did lose about half of its membership for some considerable time. Largely through his moderation, however, the SAP in the long run actually gained members. Throughout this period the Social Democrats put suffrage before all other types of reform, including education, and certainly in preference to the revolutionary Marxism of its origins.

Amidst all this turmoil the first signs of a welfare state began to appear. In 1907 old age pensions were introduced as part of a more widely intended general national insurance framework.

In the 1908 elections the SAP increased its representation in the Lower House four-fold, although the Conservatives stayed in power with the help of the farmers. The LO advocated conciliation, but as the Young Socialists wanted a general strike confrontation could no longer be avoided. Branting tried to placate the middle classes whilst the LO tried to make the strike a sudden blow rather than a war of attrition, granting exemptions to essential functions rather than completely alienating the public. In the event Sweden's general strike lasted five weeks and was a total disaster for the labour movement, the Conservative government holding firm and refusing even to negotiate until it was over. The employers' right to hire and fire was consolidated and foremen were taken out of the trade unions.

Popular movements

Alongside the political developments of the early twentieth century, Sweden saw the emergence of popular movements of a moral and spiritual nature. As with the SAP, these appeared amongst the lower strata of society, with the encouragement of middle-class leaders, and as such they contributed to the demand for universal suffrage taken up by the Liberals and carried on by the Social Democrats. There was the free church movement, set up to make provision for alternatives to the state Lutheran Church, and the temperance movement, intended to curb the Swedes' reputation for heavy drinking. There was also the labour movement, but this is dealt with extensively in Chapter 6. By the end of the first decade of the twentieth century the first two of these had achieved at least a combined presence in the lower chamber of the Riksdag that was superior to that of the Social Democrats:

Free Church	51 of 230
Temperance Movement (absolutists)	144
Social Democratic Party (SAP)	87
	(Lundkvist, 1975)

Until 1910 the majority vote election system was in use, favouring these movements, but the proportional representation brought in that year by the Conservatives went against them. This was good fortune for the Social Democrats, however, because many from the popular movements joined forces with them, only relatively few preferring the Liberals. The temperance issue was never resolved to the satisfaction of the absolutists, perhaps fortunately considering what happened during prohibition in the United States. Lundkvist (1975) reports that the deciding factor in Sweden was the potential loss of government revenue. As a typically Swedish pragmatic compromise the collection of excise was transferred from the localities to the central administration so that it could be used more constructively, for instance in education – education reform financed by a tax on liquor sales is something that appeals to the Swedish character. To this day, however, liquor in Sweden has to be purchased from the *Systembolaget* (state stores) and since 1977 even strong beer cannot be obtained from the supermarkets, which illustrates the desire to maintain the principle. Currently some medical experts advocate more restrictions on health grounds.

The demise of sovereign power and the attainment of universal suffrage

The other important political issue of the time was defence. This may appear strange for a neutral country, but neutrality has to be upheld by force if necessary and the Scandinavian countries were determined to remain neutral in the approaching Great War. Sweden had declared neutrality as early as 1834 (Scott, 1977) but it was not tested until 1914. With this in mind the Conservatives were proposing the building of three iron-clad naval vessels and it became an issue in the 1911 election, the first by proportional representation. The Liberals emerged victorious and in the first instance the King had to accept a government separate from his own beliefs. Apparently the Liberal prime minister, Staaf, had a very difficult interview with the King when he had to convince him of the rightness of change, against his protestations of loss of authority, based on his assumption that all ministers were his advisers to be chosen at will.

In 1913 the farmers had formed the *Bondeförbundet* (Agrarian) Party and added to the centre presence in Swedish politics, whilst a separate Farmers' National Association emerged closer to the Conservatives. This proved critical to the growing pressure for the defence issue to be settled. The King acceded, eager to assert his power, for one last time as it turned out, when the farmers confronted him in the Castle Courtyard Coup and prime minister Staaf, who had suffered a smear campaign in the process, resigned his *Folkpartiet* government. The Liberals advocated parliamentary rule whilst the Conservatives, with some maverick Liberal support, put defence first. As a result of this the Liberals lost much of their support, leaving two equally-sized centre/right and left-wing blocs. However, most important of all was that the tradition of the middle way and of cooperation in politics was secured, to be the uniquely Swedish way.

In 1917 shortages of food in Sweden, caused by the Scandinavian countries' isolation during the First World War, caused further unrest, demonstrations and riots. There was a demand for direct action rather than negotiations, and unemployment and increased military service pushed youth to the fore. Branting once again found himself in the position of having to restrain demands for revolution. He visited Soviet Russia soon after the Revolution, but this still did not affect his resolve to put the suffrage issue before all else. The events in Russia naturally fomented unrest in neighbouring Sweden but attempts to produce an extreme takeover of the SAP failed, as they did in Denmark, and in contrast to Norway and Finland where they succeeded and took their parties on to a different course. Lenin is reputed to have told the Young Socialists, Branting's chief protagonists, 'Branting is much smarter than you' (Andrae, 1975). It was Branting rather than the Young Socialists who thus secured widespread worker support in Sweden.

In 1917 there was formed a *Folkpartiet*/SAP government, with Nils Eden, of the former, as prime minister and Hjalmar Branting as finance minister – the first SAP government post. Branting resigned from the government in 1918, but in that same year universal suffrage for both houses of the *Riksdag* was attained at last.

The coming of Social Democratic Labour government

Lewin (1975) describes a new schism entering Swedish politics from 1918. The SAP had just begun to assert itself as a major force and found itself faced with a joint opposition of Conservatives, Liberals and Agrarians, the Conservatives standing for state intervention in a situation of conflict between capital and labour whilst the Agrarians believed in the free market mechanism as a means of finding equilibrium and harmony in society. These are the familiar conflict and consensus perspectives of social analysis. Ernst Wigforss, the Social Democrats' planner, rejected the idea that low wages could lead to high employment. Instead he took seriously Marx's theory of the tendency to under-consumption inherent in capitalist societies and, linking this with the ideas of the English liberal economists, he recommended that higher wages could remove the problem by increasing purchasing power. In an entirely different context, this was a principle taken up in the United States at the time as it pioneered a society of mass production, mass communication and mass consumption. For Sweden it was the beginnings of Keynesian economics, before Keynes himself had properly articulated them. For the opposition parties freedom meant the free market, but for the Social Democrats it meant freedom from the domination of capital, from poverty and from under-consumption (Lewin, 1975, p. 286).

During the 1920s the SAP had to content itself with working along liberal lines, but in 1928 it suffered, in the *Riksdag*, its last defeat of the twenties. In 1929, the year of the Wall Street crash, Sweden suffered an agricultural crisis which also affected industry. Things got worse and by 1931 the country had to leave the gold standard and had 250,000 unemployed. The SAP in 1930 began making statements about 'productive state work and wages set by contract agreement', heralding the introduction of their policies proper – the plans of Wigforss.

Thus it was that the SAP came to power in 1932, with Per Albin Hansson, the successor to Hjalmar Branting, as prime minister and Ernst Wigforss as finance minister, with promises of urban help for unemployed workers and loans for the farmers. This was known as the 'crisis agreement', and there were equivalents at the same time in Norway and Denmark. Agriculture was certainly a theme of the politics of this period, without detracting from Sweden's continuing industrial advances; from 1932 agricultural associations began to appear for dairy products, meat marketing and eggs, and they provided powerful interest groups. In 1936 there was even a brief, caretaker *Bondeförbundet* Party government – the 'red/green' coalition; Hansson remained as prime minister but with four *Bondeförbundet* ministers.

Throughout the thirties the SAP confirmed its abandonment of revolutionary principles by pursuing policies of welfare reform and the control of investment. Wigforss and members of the 'Stockholm School' of economics, such as Gunnar Myrdal, who became better known outside Sweden than Wigforss himself, laid down the foundations for the developments to come. From 1938 the Social Services Commission, an example of the devolved government that was to become so prevalent in Sweden, presided over the foundation of the welfare state until 1951, when it was superseded by a whole range of public bodies. However the wider adoption of a combination of state infrastructure and public ownership of industry had to wait until after the Second World War.

The Second World War

Sweden's maintenance of neutrality during the Second World War, against the background of the German occupation of Denmark and Norway, was an important watershed for the nation. The feelings can perhaps be a little better understood by reference to the speech by Per Edvin Skold to the *Riksdag* in June 1942, as quoted by Molin (1975, p. 305):

Sweden is the point of departure for all of our efforts . . .
Without an independent Sweden, our efforts are ended. If we
wish to improve social conditions, if we wish to work for peace
on earth, if wish to create a society that is better in this or that
respect, then first and foremost we must have a free place to
work, where we can make full use of our powers. This place is
Sweden, and in order to preserve it there is in fact no limit to the
sacrifice we ought to take upon us.

This gives some idea of the way in which neutrality is linked with progress. The SAP is not by any means a nationalist party, as the phrase is normally understood, although the preservation of the base for progress and the identification of this with the Swedish nation is certainly a special form of nationalism.

The Skagerack blockade, following the German occupation of Denmark and Norway, was a blow to the Swedish economy. It reduced imports by a half and exports by one-third. In fact the years of 1940 and 1941 were years of famine and, from a position of industrial growth, the country went to one of decline. By 1944 the production index was 12 per cent below what it had been in 1939 (Molin, 1975). From 1942 wages and prices had to be frozen and some foods were subsidised to keep prices down. Defence spending brought taxes up to the level of most other European countries, which was a turning point for Sweden that was not to be reversed in peace time – on issues of allocation policy, in a fashion that has become typically Swedish, it is accepted that for the lowest to stand still the highest has to lose.

There are aspects of the neutrality which it is difficult for outsiders to understand. In 1940 Sweden rejected requests from England and France to permit the transport of troops to Finland, which was at war with Russia, at that time honouring a non-aggression pact with Germany. A little later, however, Sweden did agree to allow the Germans to transport troops and war materials on its railway line from Norway to the ferry-crossing to Denmark at Elsinore. The trains were patrolled by armed Swedish troops and the Germans were not allowed to carry arms. Then, in 1941 the German Engelbrecht Division was transported from Norway to Finland on the Swedish railways; by this time Russia had joined the Allies and these Germans were bound for the eastern front.

For the Swedes this all represented the narrow and delicate pathway between neutrality and occupation. As long as the Germans could obtain their demands, and given that it would have been costly for them to invade Sweden, the Swedes' neutrality, and their base for progress, could be preserved. To this day the Swedes maintain their armed forces on the basis of a calculated prohibitive cost to an aggressor of invasion. During the War the Coalition government preserved a fine balance, restricting for instance printed material of either a pro-Nazi or an anti-Nazi nature. According to Molin (1975, p. 322), the protection of Sweden was more important at the time than the protection of democracy.

There can be little doubt, however, that for the most part Swedish sympathies were with the Allies. There were some moves in the beginning, when it looked as though Germany might win the War, to take the German side, but these did not enjoy popular support. In fact Sweden provided a haven for all kinds of fugitives from the Nazis; in particular, Denmark's threatened Jews were almost all smuggled across the Öresund to safety. With permission from the British, Sweden continued to supply Germany with high-grade iron ore and ball-bearings, only slowly reducing the supply to a half by 1944. However, by this time fast motor-boats could beat the blockade to bring ball-bearings to Britain. At the height of the threat of a German invasion of Sweden, in 1943, there was reported to be a great feeling of cooperation in the face of adversity; Samuelsson (1968) refers to this as 'new acquaintanceships' between people from all walks of life.

The 'golden age'

The period after the Second World War, with Swedish industry in full ascendancy and the SAP consistently in government, up to the beginning of the recession in the early seventies, is seen as a 'golden age' for Sweden. This was the period when all sections of Swedish society came to realise, in concrete terms, their outstanding success as an advanced industrial nation. People linked this success with SAP government and its concord with labour, so that even hard-headed businessmen came to see the advantages.

Initially, after the war, two significant bodies were set up to generate plans for recovery. The first was a government commission, the Myrdal Commission; the second was an SAP/LO body put together to formulate the 'labour movement's post-war pro-gramme'. Some individuals were members of both. They had a common effect, too, in advocating more government intervention, leading to the realisation of the publicly-controlled infrastructure that is such a distinct feature of the Swedish mixed economy, retaining nevertheless a high proportion – 90 to 95 per cent – of private ownership of industry. A wage-freeze was operated at first and, with inflation as the main problem, price control. Always, however, full employment was the primary goal and, with a view to this, interventionary policy was above all directed at investment. Thus the Meidner Plan – an initiative in the 1980s to direct a proportion of profits directly into investment under the control of the labour movement, the so-called Wage-Earner Funds (*Löntagar-fonder*) – must be seen as the culmination of decades of planning in this direction.

The SAP prime minister between 1946 and 1968, Tage Erlander, adopted the precedent of informal meetings between influential businessmen, labour leaders and politicians at the official residence at Harpsund. In the Swedish social democratic tradition, whilst professing to be a Marxist, he was a great believer in compromise and consensus, and these meetings provided another dimension to the already decentralised Swedish politics. More than that, the example set by these meetings came to be known as the 'spirit of Harpsund'.

The welfare state

Probably the greatest achievement for Sweden during this time was the elimination of poverty through the extension of the welfare state. Jones (1976) describes the thirties as providing the bare necessities, the sixties as providing welfare as a right and the seventies putting the emphasis on prevention. Walter Korpi, probably the most well-known observer of this process outside Sweden, puts the emphasis on the reform of old-age pensions. In 1948 their real value was trebled (Korpi, 1975) and since the 1950s it has increased more rapidly than the real wage for industrial workers (Korpi, 1976, p. 136). He asserts that 'the greatest success of social policy in post-war Sweden has undoubtedly been the raising of the standard of living of persons on old-age pensions, which has dramatically reduced the more serious forms of poverty among the old' (Korpi, 1976, p. 145). By this method, of course, income is redistributed along the life-cycle toward old age, rather than between individuals – 'pressures from poverty have thus been eased among the old while they have increased among the young' (Korpi, 1976, p. 131).

Therefore there is still a need for support elsewhere and Korpi (1975) draws attention to Sweden's payment of 'social assistance'. This is something that Swedish law guarantees for people in need but

Table 1.2 **Rowntree's cycle showing periods of deprivation**

Stage	Deprivation/plenty
Childhood	deprivation
Young single adults	plenty
Married couples without dependent children	plenty
Married couples with dependent children	deprivation
Elderly married couples without dependent children	plenty
Old age	deprivation

(after Rowntree, 1941)

for which means tests are administered by social boards in the *Kommunen* (district councils), the smallest administrative unit in Swedish local government. Korpi argues that the profile of social assistance in Sweden in the early post-war years conforms well to Rowntree's (the pioneering English social reformer) classic 'periods of deprivation'. The highest incidence of payment in Sweden according to demand proved, on inspection, to be to the equivalents of the 'deprived' categories in Rowntree's cycle shown in Table 1.2. In fact social assistance payments declined over the years of the 'golden age' and this has to be taken as an index of national affluence and a reflection of the realisation of full employment according to government policy. The following figures show social assistance as a percentage of all social policy expenditure in Sweden:

1945	16%	
1950	4%	
Since	1–2%	(Korpi, 1975)

Not everyone applies for social assistance – there is some stigma attached even in progressive Sweden. However, everyone over the age of sixteen is regarded as independent and so young single adults, supposedly affluent according to the cycle, are not excluded from claiming, and in the later period of the 1960s and 1970s they became a large group of claimants, although in a much reduced overall group.

Korpi concludes that social policy affects 'structural' factors more than 'releasing' factors. 'Structural' factors refer to the tendencies described above, whereas 'releasing' factors are cases of decreased income with perhaps increased costs, as in cases of illness, unemployment, divorce, bereavement, etc.; the latter are relatively neglected – 'where the normal income from work is low, social policy reforms have done little to ameliorate the situation' (Korpi, 1976, p. 146). It is much more difficult to deal equitably with personal variations in affluence and poverty than with generalised variations over an entire population, and this is, of course, common to all welfare programmes.

Many people have decried what they like to describe as Sweden's 'cradle to the grave' programme, but in some ways it is in fact not as extensive as the British system. It is another question entirely as to whether the quality of service is higher in Sweden and the waiting-lists shorter, but on such things as doctors' fees the Swedes get only two-thirds refunded whilst medicines, except for certain vital ones, and dental treatment are cheap rather than free. On the other hand every day of sickness is paid, and in case of unemployment a certain level of income is guaranteed relating to previous earnings, of which the range is greater than that operated in Britain.

Health care has developed exclusively as a state activity without an alternative private sector for the well-off. The middle-class, never having achieved any real ascendancy in Sweden, threw in their lot with this and the result is a level of service which could hardly be surpassed. Sweden currently spends twice as much per capita on its health service than does the United Kingdom. Hospitals have traditionally been a province of government activity (Samuelsson, 1975) but new hospitals like the one at Sundsvall, opened in 1975, are equipped to the last degree, every bit as impressive as the most lavishly endowed private hospital in America, but under state ownership and control. Within this hospital it is possible to see the characteristically Swedish pattern of administration taking place with representatives of political parties and interest groups amongst those that monitor the day-to-day running of the establishment.

In housing Sweden has to be able to provide for all – the climate is too severe for anything else. The *Kommunen* (district councils) provide flats for almost everyone, if necessary, including, perhaps especially, the most recent immigrants. Often it is done in conjunction with the housing cooperatives which are a feature of Sweden. Low-cost loans for furniture are also provided when this is a problem. In the private sector, too, new homes come equipped not only to withstand the severe winters but also with a whole range of appliances, right up to a dish-washer. Many Swedes have a private sauna too.

Since about 1960 there has been considerable discussion about whether Swedish concerns for social welfare are humanitarian or born out a love for tidiness and cleanliness. Books such as *A Clean Well-Lighted Place*, by the Englishwoman Cathleen Knott (1961), attempt to argue the latter. The feeling is that in establishing their neat and tidy society and welfare cocoon the Swedes have lost something along the way and are, on the whole, dull. This, it would appear, is to confuse physical neatness and self-discipline, as Swedish national traits, with over-conformity. Rather, the security and satisfaction inherent in Swedish society give Swedes the confidence to go out and 'do their own thing' both individually and, nationally, through international relations. Such writers are oblivious to the satisfaction Swedes get from being a part of the progressiveness, from taking a stand against the ills of the world and from holding firm to the belief that there is a better way of arranging society which Sweden can find the way to. Such a view is well expressed in Lars Gustafsson's (1964) book, *The Public Dialogue In Sweden.*

Education and society

By comparison with other countries, there is much greater interchange in Sweden between the universities and industry or the state administration. It is quite usual for Swedes to transfer from university posts to business or to the civil service, and back again in many cases. It is here, if anywhere, that the Swedish equivalent of the 'old boy network' operates. A select group from the universities, latterly with PhDs, circulate in government, civil service, industry and the unions. Inasmuch as they are predominantly supporters of the Social Democratic Party, it is felt that the old party hierarchy, with a realistic feel for the working-class roots, has been replaced by a meritocracy and that Sweden has truly become an achievement society, although one with a new form of élitism.

Additionally, there are many semi-independent but government-sponsored institutions which employ staff at the same level as the universities and which are engaged in research of various kinds. Examples of these are *Statskontöret*, the civil service's agency of social science research, and SIFO, the state agency for opinion polls. These tend to be much more extensive than in other countries and reflect the Swedes' enthusiasm for expert opinion in the various government decision-making processes. Part of this is to do with the way that the social sciences have developed in Sweden. Sociology, for instance, has tended to stress methodological accuracy rather than social critique. It has therefore relatively easily acquired administrative application in the role of provider of data for the state. Sociologists in government departments have taken part in policy formation to an extent that is unheard of in Britain. As an example, the literature on social mobility, including élite mobility, in Sweden is probably the most extensive in the world, but by contrast, there are almost no studies of Swedish industrialisation (Scase, 1976a).

As will be described in the chapter on politics and industry (Chapter 7), central government administration, in the strict sense, is tiny and extensive use is made of boards and commissions which collect information for negotiation, between interested parties, of decisions which will affect the whole society. These bodies have a voracious appetite for data. Perhaps the key to this greater integration between the academic world and the polity is the fact that in general there is less of a gulf between general values and the values of intellectuals than in most countries outside Scandinavia, and certainly much less than in Britain. This makes for a greater harmony between, as it were, 'town and gown' and a greater general acceptance of academic ideas. At the level of school education Sweden works universally on a comprehensive system. Not that it was ahead of other countries in this respect. The original proposal for changeover to comprehensives was in 1948, but the present system was not introduced until 1969, after experiments from 1950 to 1962. However when it was instituted it was done so throughout Sweden and with a high level of support from all quarters – it had been tried, discussed thoroughly by all parties, and they were determined to make a go of it.

At that time, incidentally when the SAP leader Olof Palme was Minister of Education, the percentage of the working-class going to university had only reached 20 per cent, less than Britain and considerably less than the USA. Harnquist and Bengtsson usefully summarise the system as incorporated:

> Sweden provides compulsory education of nine years for all
> children between the ages of seven and sixteen. This takes place
> within the context of the comprehensive school and with a
> curriculum determined nationally by the Minister of Education.
> The school is divided into three stages: grades one to three, four
> to six and seven to nine. English, as the first foreign language, is
> introduced in grade three and is compulsory until grade nine. The
> second foreign language – French or German – is taken in grades
> seven to nine with art, economy and technology providing
> alternative choices. The only formal 'streaming' that takes place
> within this system is in the study of mathematics and foreign
> languages when, in grades seven, eight and nine instruction is
> given at two levels of difficulty. (Härnquist and Bengtsson, 1976,
> pp. 206–7)

Additionally, there is at least one year's nursery education before school. Playschools are organised in the localities and one house on an estate may be turned over to this purpose; the housing cooperatives make this easy to arrange. Then from age seven to fourteen truly comprehensive education takes place, with English taught as the main foreign language from age nine. Between ages fourteen and sixteen there is an element of re-grouping and this can be followed by two years' vocational instruction or three to four years of preparation for higher education.

To the outside observer there is a great deal of 'Swedish propaganda' in the schools. It is equivalent to 'American propaganda' in American schools, although since the demise of the British Empire this phenomenon is not apparent in UK schools. In the Swedish case it dwells upon the advantages of the country and, in contrast to America, its achievements in the social and, to a lesser extent, industrial spheres. It certainly features a collective rather than an individualistic perspective, and yet it is apparent that the individual does get a great deal of attention in Sweden. It will be argued elsewhere that the collective achievements of Sweden do give the individual confidence to go out and do his or her own thing.

Perhaps the most revealing observation that the above writers make is that the system causes educational decisions to be postponed until 'an age when the pupils' own interests and capacities would be more likely to play a decisive role than the expectations and aspirations of the parents' (Härnquist and Bengtsson, 1976, pp. 207). This is a highly individualistic stance. Prior to the 1969 reforms, Sweden's profiles were similar to other countries in terms of the position of parents' influence on attainment – there was a high correlation between educational attainment and social background. However, with a view to possible emulation of this, it is difficult to envisage many countries, or perhaps more importantly many political parties, getting away with explicit policies designed to take away choice from parents and give it to their children of school age. On the other hand students in higher education in Sweden are financed only by loans, or if they are lucky scholarships, and there are no statutory grants. This must certainly have some bearing on the propensity for working-class children to proceed into higher education.

The Swedes have a reputation for being serious-minded, and this certainly emerges in their attitude to self-improvement after school. The long winter evenings are for study; even television, which in Sweden is kept relatively educational in any case, has not entirely changed things. The Swedish Cooperative Movement, *Kooperative Förbunda* (KF), began workers' study circles, similar to the Workers' Educational Association in England but nowadays certainly more widespread, in the late nineteenth century. In addition the LO trade unions run study circles intended to involve their members in the union's work and its relationship to the development of the society, as will be discussed further in Chapter 6. These are high-sounding objectives, but interest and attendance is higher than British unions could ever hope to achieve in current circumstances. In summer, however, which in Sweden is short, sweet and to be enjoyed, the self-improvement turns to ideals of physical fitness. Tennis has received a tremendous boost in the wake of Björn Borg and Mats Wilander and, in terms of general relaxation, the Swedes spend more per head on holidays than any other nation on earth (Jones, 1976).

Social differences

Social differences in Sweden today undoubtedly exist, but they are lessened by the homogeneity of the society – for instance the language differences between north and south are quite small compared with many countries – and by the tremendous advances that have been made in living standards. The percentage of the working class in higher education is, as has already been stated, nowadays equal to that in Britain, although below that of the USA and Japan, and social mobility is high (Tomasson, 1970; Erikson, 1976). Parental ambition tends to be high, too. The Swedes are renowned for their high readership of 'quality' newspapers, and 90 per cent of the population vote in general elections (Tomasson, 1970; Johannson, 1976). All classes are well dressed, one in four Swedes own cars, as compared with one in three Americans, and their ownership of telephones and television sets is again only surpassed by the US (Tomasson, 1970).

Sweden probably contains the world's highest incidence of second homes, though this is not just an index of affluence. Only a few generations ago the Swedes were almost exclusively country dwellers. Firstly, as they moved into industrial jobs and different locations, this left Swedish families with second homes from their immediate past. Secondly, they have inherited a love, some would say need, for nature which leads them to keep and maintain these second homes. Most Swedes want to move to the country or the forest when they emerge from their long, harsh winter, just as during the winter most Swedes want to ski. Keeping fit is a national obsession; the Vasa long-distance, cross-country ski race attracts an entry of thousands and Ingemar Stenmark, several times world champion in downhill and slalom events, is a national hero.

Swedish law prevents the erecting of fences, except for safety reasons, because it is believed that everyone should have the right to wander where the fancy takes them. The ideal is to have a house that backs on to the forest so that you can go off direct from your back door either on foot or on skis, according to the season. New housing developments are, where possible built this way and, since land is in fairly plentiful supply in all but the inner urban areas, it is not unusual.

Tomasson (1970) argues that privacy is a prime feature of the Swedish character. Garbo's famed 'I want to be alone' posture is taken as a generalised trait. According to him, people do not 'drop in' on each other and there is a strong preference for private accommodation amongst office-workers in their work, students in their accommodation, etc. The reserve of Swedes is, in these terms, captured in an old joke about the two Norwegians, the two Danes and the two Swedes stranded on a desert island. The Danes form a cooperative, the Norwegians fight and the Swedes wait to be introduced.

What goes with this is caution and an abhorrence of violence which translates in the area of productive activity to a preference for the aesthetic component and the quality of the product. Swedish design has been successful not only for its engineering but also for its style, and this is reflected in the nation's export record. In a similar fashion, aspects of the national character emerge as a kind of international social conscience. Swedish intervention as a neutral nation in world affairs is really quite vigorous and often attracts strong criticism from the 'super-powers'.

Amongst all this liberalism, one would expect to find an ideological commitment to anti-racism. It is certainly there and the Swedes are quick to condemn countries such as South Africa for their abhorrent policies. On the other hand, the principle has never been exhaustively tested amongst the mass of Swedish society. There have been some less-than-ideal episodes with concentrations of Turkish immigrants in Sweden. Only the extremely limited coverage of international news in the English newspapers has kept these incidents from the general attention of English people, in their own agonised concern about the problems of English racial prejudice.

At the end of this process of development we see in Sweden a decentralised market economy dominated by private enterprise, but with ambitious state policy in public consumption and public saving, including income redistribution, in a publicly-owned infrastructure designed to maximise harmony and in a policy of stabilisation. This liberal and democratic welfare state thus operates in a mixed economy and has produced a high capacity to innovate, even against a background of inflationary, high-employment economic policy (Tomasson, 1970; Lindbeck 1975). For many people outside Sweden this is a very enviable state of affairs.

The great strength of SAP politics is their link with Sweden's material success. As will be mentioned elsewhere, the strongest corroboration of this is the tendency for hard-headed businessmen to feel at least nervous about a change of government in case 'it kills the goose that lays the golden eggs'. The length of the terms of power of SAP governments has generated huge confidence amongst the Swedes in their ability to find a better way to arrange life in an advanced industrial nation. As Himmelstrand and Lindhagen (1976, pp. 229–30) point out, the SAP was linked with the beginning of this progress, as it is now with the pay-off.

2 Industry and technology

Sweden is the major innovator of the Scandinavian countries and, throughout the period of its transition to an industrial society has displayed a remarkable capacity for innovation. During the seventeenth and eighteenth centuries there were many pioneers of this tradition. Polhem (1661–1751) was an all-round innovator, sometimes referred to as the 'Swedish Leonardo da Vinci', whilst Celsius (1701–44) has given his name to the temperature scale. Linnaeus (1707–78) is well known as a biologist, while Clydenius was the 'Swedish Adam Smith' but preceded him (Scott, 1977). And there are many more, though seldom heard of outside of Sweden. The Academy of Science at the University of Uppsala was established in 1728 and the Royal Swedish Academy of Science in Stockholm in 1739.

The nation's considerable reserves of timber and iron ore gave rise to technology in order to exploit them, and this expertise was successfully transferred into other areas. Amongst the inventions which have been turned into prodigious export earners are the steam turbine, the centrifugal separator, as used in the dairy industry, the modern ball-bearing, the adjustable spanner, the safety match, the air compressor and precision instruments of various kinds (Lindbeck, 1975, p. 5). This has all been potentiated by liberal, market-orientated economic policies, working through a private sector, backed up by an elaborate publicly-operated infrastructure, in an atmosphere of 150 years of peace, accompanied by a calm labour market (Lindbeck, 1975, p. 7).

Despite the reputation for innovation and for the continual renewal of the industrial infrastructure, actual research and development spending in Sweden is quite modest. During the seventies it ran at 1.2 per cent of GDP, as compared with 2.1 per cent in the United Kingdom and 2.7 per cent in the United States. According to Jones' (1976) analysis of planning and productivity in Sweden, this must mean that such research and development as is undertaken must be better directed. The Swedes are good at problem-solving and they like to experiment. The experimental use of statistics has been applied to such things as the cost of shop-lifting as compared to the benefits of a life of petty crime, and the cost of national defence as compared with the cost of invasion for an aggressor. In the business sphere the same principle is illustrated by the way that the Swedes have carved out an impressive market in computer software. When they latch on to something like this the gross investment in the enterprise is very high, with finance available not only from private sources but also from investment funds, elements of profits which have to be set aside for investment, the state pension fund, which is directed to invest in new technology, and perhaps in the future from the *Löntagarfonder* (wage earner funds). All of these will be described in more detail in Chapters 6 and 7.

At the same time, in Sweden there is a preference for multi-disciplinary planning so that not just economics are involved but social and environmental factors too. Thus subsidies to industry to reduce pollution, for instance, are an integral part of economic planning. This principle applies in other areas as well, such as when huge waiting lists for the allocation of apartments built up during the 1960s; these were reduced by increasing the rents while at the same time subsidising the poorer families. Market mechanisms and planning are used as far as possible in unison (Lindbeck, 1975).

The companies and inventions of the late nineteenth century

In the nineteenth century the government was responsible for large basic investments in communications, especially in the railways, for the transport of Swedish exports to the ports of the Baltic and the North Sea coast of Norway, and in education, especially technological education at a higher level as described in the last chapter. At the same time entrepreneurs emerged from the merchant houses of Sweden that dated back to the time when Sweden was a great maritime and mercantilist power – the Riksbank had been established as early as 1668 for these purposes. These entrepreneurs invested in timber and saw-mills, iron mining and manufacturing, and in the technology that came with them. The achievements were the result of a combination in which merchants were the financiers and technicians were the innovators. Foreign capital, too, played a part, mainly in the form of advances against orders, demonstrating the keenness of overseas buyers to obtain Swedish timber and iron. By 1856, however, the Wallenbergs, Sweden's famous banking family, had founded the Stockholms Enskilda Bank, since merged into the Scandinaviska Enskilda Bank (Scott, 1977). In addition English technicians were imported to develop textile manufacturing, railway construction and some aspects of engineering (Jörberg, 1975).

Although Sweden industrialised late by comparison with the rest of Europe and the United States, the joint-stock company was adopted on a widespread basis from the 1870s, about the same time as in Britain. This form of company became the biggest employer very quickly and by 1912 was employing 80 per cent of the labour force (Jörberg, 1975).

Jörberg (1975) describes how the initial industrial boom of the 1870s brought large profits from exports which were transformed into capital for industry. With the government-sponsored expansion of the railways, transport costs fell, marketing became easier and raw materials and fuel became cheaper. The relocation of population and the establishment of new settlements was made easier by the improvements in travel and in the standard of living. This follows the pattern of industrialisation in other countries, but at the same time Sweden managed to avoid large sprawling industrial conurbations. With the exception of Stockholm, Gothenburg and Malmö the towns were relatively small and, overall, the population was well dispersed.

During the period from 1880 to 1914 the progress continued and Swedish exports increased one and a half times (Jörberg, 1975). Behind all this Sweden became an established industrial nation, with the social and political progress described for the period in the previous chapter. Timber exports remained, but were joined by the more profitable and labour-intensive paper products from the pulp-mills and furniture from carpentry factories. The indoor existence, forced upon Scandinavians by the climate for much of the year, ensured an interest in furniture which has made their design world-famous. The exports of iron were augmented by those of high-grade iron ore for the steel-works of Europe, which were entering into new phases of mass production as the second industrial revolution, involving electricity, chemicals and the internal combustion engine, gathered momentum. Most important of all, Sweden began to produce its own engineering products, born of its own producer technology. This was not emulation; from the 1890s the Swedish engineering industry entered its own new phase of development with Swedish inventions. Towards the end of the nineteenth century half of the steel production was retained, a significant index of Sweden's own industrialisation.

Lars Magnus Ericsson produced the first table telephone, founded the L.M. Ericsson Company in 1876 and began manufacturing the equipment for Sweden's own telecommunications network. But he did not stop there; factories were set up in several countries, as Sweden set out on an impressive, for the size of the country, foreign investment programme. There was a factory in England at Nottingham, since taken over by Plessey. Nevertheless, in 1985 it was announced that Ericsson's AXE digital switching system had been selected to work alongside British Telecom's own System X in the British telecommunications system. Ericsson is nowadays the leader of Sweden's electronics industry and its Alfaskop microcomputers are advertised world-wide. It is Sweden's second biggest employer overall, with 74,000 people, nearly 40,000 of whom are employed abroad. The foreign investment is still very significant, although Ericsson now rates fourth after Volvo, Electrolux and ASEA.

In the field of domestic equipment Gustaf Dalen was a pioneer in the use of gas and founded the Aga Company, which also produced lighthouse equipment. Baltzar von Platen invented the gas-driven refrigerator without moving parts and this was exploited by the Electrolux Company, now a household word, to the extent that most of its customers abroad never realise that it is a Swedish company. Electrolux is Sweden's biggest employer overall, although 60,000 of its 89,500 workers are abroad, reflecting the level of its overseas investment. Sweden is not in the EEC and so has to set up factories in the EEC countries in order to avoid disadvantageous duties on consumer-durable products and thereby be able to compete effectively. As well as its own plants, Electrolux now controls the successful Italian manufacturer Zanussi. The policies seem to work, for Electrolux is consistently listed in Sweden's top ten most profitable companies.

Sven Wingquist perfected the modern ball-bearing and the SKF Company was founded in 1907. With its multiplicity of applications in the products of the advanced industrial nations, it was sure to succeed. Indeed its output became so indispensable to European industry that during the Second World War it found itself, as a neutral nation, supplying the munitions factories of both sides. Like the other companies already mentioned, SKF has become a large foreign investor and exporter and a consistently profitable company.

Gustaf de Laval developed the cream separator in 1878 and the steam turbine in 1890. The separator enabled the mechanisation of the dairy industry to take place, not only for Sweden's own numerous dairy farmers but also for the world's dairy industries. The steam turbine revolutionised the powering of ships, power stations and other applications requiring large amounts of power. As with those firms mentioned above, the Alfa-Laval Company became a big foreign investor for Sweden, as well as a considerable exporter.

The common theme running through all these impressive company histories is the high added-value potential for the product and its suitability for exporting. When aggregated, the achievements represent a solid foundation for Sweden's economic progress. According to Jones (1976, p. 10), 'without appreciating these, the present status of the Swedish economy would resemble the accomplishments of a magician rather than the result of determined creative action by many people'.

In all of this a more intensive use of plant and capital per worker was achieved and, to protect the achievement, a protectionist tariff was instigated. In the first phase of its progress the Social Democratic Labour Party (SAP), under its far-sighted leader, Hjalmar Branting, was well aware of the implications and sought, by negotiation and, in the first place, the establishment of universal suffrage, to get a better deal for the workers. In the long run, however, they were to do this by increasing collaboration with the capitalists rather than by obstruction. The phases of the Saltsjöbaden agreement, of co-determination and, ultimately, of the *Löntagarfonder* (wage-earner funds) are described in more detail in Chapters 6 and 7.

Volvo and Saab

No account of Sweden's industrial development would be complete without mention of the incredible success of these two vehicle manufacturing concerns. It is an achievement in itself that such a relatively small country should be able to maintain a vehicle industry at all, given the domination of the giant producers on the present scene. Yet not only do Volvo and Saab require no government support, they are two of the most profitable companies in Sweden. A drive down any motorway in Europe will reveal that a large proportion of the lorries and coaches encountered have chassis, if not complete vehicles, from Volvo or Saab-Scania. Both firms produce up-market cars, yet consistently manage to be included amongst the biggest sellers in the major markets. Both have built up a reputation based on safety and can justifiably claim to be the only volume car manufacturer who genuinely build in safety as one of the foremost features of their development programmes.

Volvo is Sweden's biggest foreign investor, biggest exporter, biggest employer, best wage-payer and most profitable company. It continues to break its own records and yet cannot keep up with demand, even in its prime export market, America. Its position is so strong that it can choose its operations, currently extracting itself from oil trading in the face of poor performance (a high proportion of Sweden's biggest loss-makers are in the oil business). Meanwhile it pursues interests in the food industry. Volvo's more recent successes have been under the leadership of Pehr Gyllenhammar, an influential voice in Sweden and elsewhere.

Saab began as an aircraft manufacturer and, remarkably, continues to be one, albeit with help from Volvo, quite apart from its car and truck manufacturing. This is an achievement in itself. The cost of developing a modern front-line military aircraft is so high that, outside the USA and the USSR, only France and Sweden have continued to do so on their own. Saab supplies the Swedish Air Force with its Viggen aircraft and during the 1970s wanted to supply the Indian Air Force as well. Due to the fact that its jet engine is produced by Volvo under licence from an American manufacturer, the Carter administration refused to let the deal go through, given India's non-aligned stance and friendship with the USSR. This was extremely annoying for Saab because the Viggen is expensive to produce, given its relatively short production run and lack of operational competitiveness with the latest American and European equivalent productions, and the Indian order would have improved the arithmetic.

Both firms have introduced revolutionary production techniques in the interests of making work in a car factory more tolerable. By 1968 the labour turnover at Volvo had reached 33 per cent and absenteeism was of the order of one in seven, calculated to have resulted in 20 per cent excess manning and an annual retraining cost of £8 million per annum (Jones, 1976), whilst at Saab the turnover on some lines was as high as 70 per cent. It was the latter firm, therefore, that began in 1969 to involve the workers at its Södertälje plant in the consideration and planning of more congenial methods of working. Small groups were set up to plan such methods, meeting together at regular intervals, and working together to produce a visible end product. Not all of the experiments were successful, but by 1973 the system was operational. It consists basically of loops in the production line which allow for some choice of method and pace, and for variations such as training programmes (Jones, 1976, p. 116). Fluctuations in production, usually upwards in Saab's case, can be accommodated and although the system is basically less efficient in straightforward production terms, this is counteracted by reduced disruption and increased worker satisfaction. It has been calculated that job stoppages at Saab were reduced from 6 per cent to 2.2 per cent of production time and that labour turnover on the unpopular chassis line went from 72 per cent in 1969 to 20 per cent in 1972 (Jones, 1976).

At Volvo, Pehr Gyllenhammer's philosophy is that society is producing, simultaneously, better educated people and simpler jobs, and that this just does not make sense. Therefore, the job content was increased, first at the Skovde engine plant in 1972 and then at the show-piece Kalmar car plant opened in 1974. The latter was intended to be the major step towards manufacturing a quality product based on the concept of meaning in work (Jones, 1976). The site at Kalmar, on the Baltic coast south of Stockholm, was chosen by the Labour Market Board (an instrument of devolved government including representatives of employers and all types of worker) because it was a pocket of unemployment. Additionally, reflecting the fact that Swedish idealism is nearly always braced with pragmatism, it was an area without previous experience of production line work. It has to be accepted that it is a case of Swedish business taking steps that others would baulk at, admittedly in favourable circumstances. The capital costs at Kalmar were about 10 per cent more than in a conventional installation, but this turned out to be against a background in which Volvo was increasing its turnover by 70 per cent in three years whilst maintaining a return on total assets of around 12 per cent. Profits after tax in 1973 were £25 million. Not that Kalmar was to be allowed any special privileges – it had to pay off right from the start (Jones, 1976).

In 1975 production was put under the control of computers. This may seem a contradiction in a plant designed to enhance the human element, but the computer element, apart from coordinating the tedious matching of components, is designed to fulfil the fetching and carrying by means of robot trucks. This enabled the factory to be designed without the constraints of a production line, thus producing an atmosphere of small workshops. It is a modernistic hexagonal building with many windows and an emphasis on personal space (Jones, 1976). The large stores required for a car factory are located away from the production bays, producing a lack of clutter. The robot carriers are electric and glide silently through the factory, which in any case has extra sound insulation. The small groups, about fifteen workers in each, are responsible not only for their own organisation, in the true human relations school tradition, but also for their own internal quality control. In this set-up the computer channels components and issues instructions for assembly, but it is regarded as advising the workers, who have the ultimate responsibility for the quality of the product. The plant was designed to produce 30,000 cars with single-shift working (Jones, 1976). It has attracted interest, and criticism, from all parts of the world; visiting car workers from the USA were unimpressed (Childs, 1980, p. 38). Undeterred, Volvo has gone from strength to strength, losing less production from strikes than any car manufacturer in the West. They began the experiment on the upward path and they have continued in that direction ever since.

It is significant that in 1972 it was the Employers' Association, SAF, which published guidelines to help and encourage other firms in setting up work-groups on the Volvo-Kalmar model, despite the fact that this type of plant cost on average 10 per cent more to install (Jones, 1976).

The Swedish cooperative movement

An important alternative source of manufacturing and distribution emerged at the turn of the century. This was the Swedish cooperative movement, *Kooperative Förbundet*, or KF for short. It was modelled on the Rochdale pioneers' movement in England but, whereas the latter failed to establish a manufacturing base, KF provided the Swedish working class with important alternatives to the capitalist monopolies in rubber tyres, electric light-bulbs and margarine. In addition it provided a sounder system of distribution for all commodities through its wholesale and retail structure, known today as Konsum and Domus, as indeed did its English forbear.

Today it ranks with Volvo, Electrolux, Ericsson and Saab-Scania as Sweden's fifth biggest company in terms of turnover, and it is the ninth most profitable. It has diversified into brewing, flour-milling, furniture and clothes, as well as into travel with the Reso Agency, which sends so many leisure-loving Swedes on holiday. It is associated, via the labour movement, with the OK petrol stations, currently ailing badly in common with most of the oil business in Sweden, with the Folksam Insurance Group and with the HSB housing cooperatives.

Strengths of Swedish industry

The watchword in any overview of Swedish industrial achievement is growth. Over the past 100 years Sweden's industrial growth rate is second only to Japan's, yet between 1870 and 1910 Sweden lost almost a fifth of its population in emigration to the USA. Furthermore, this growth is export-based; it is not limited to a small section of industry but is characteristic of most Swedish industry. Of course, as a small nation in terms of population the export performance is essential for the economies of scale, given the limitations of the home market. Sweden was, in fact, export orientated from the start and, as mentioned earlier, was an early exporter, to the rest of Europe in general, and to Britain in particular, of oats, timber and iron. From these propitious beginnings the range of manufactures described above, including quality steel, sophisticated machinery of several types, ships, aircraft, cars, trains and consumer durables, has been developed.

Jones (1976) draws attention to the reputation for fast modernisation that Sweden has achieved for itself. Management has been skilful, particularly in moving into premium product areas with maximum scope for export earnings. The industrial climate, which will be discussed at length in Chapter 6, has of course been favourable. The collaboration between government boards, employers and unions has ensured that changes into new technologies have gone ahead with the minimum of problems. High productivity has consistently been the norm, and with 50 per cent of Swedish industry concentrated in engineering – no longer a guarantee of success, as can be seen from the British case – the results have been truly remarkable; Swedish engineering exports have been maintained at around 45 per cent of the output by value.

Perhaps one of the most fundamental strengths of Swedish industry is the combination of flexibility at the institutional level with the respect for self-discipline and expert opinion at the individual level. Swedish organisations avoid some of the rigidity and 'calcification' that characterises so much of the industrial structure world-wide, whilst ideas of equality are usually tempered with the authority of expert opinion. Swedes tend to put less emphasis on individual achievement but the work ethic is important and this tends to result in greater group and, extrapolated further, national achievement. There is less moral judgment and more humanitarian concern, which is closely related to the belief in progress which has characterised so much of the development of Swedish society. As Tomasson (1970, p. 285) puts it, 'the past was not good because Sweden was poor' but now things are much better. Yet Swedes appear to have less sheer dependency on the material benefits of progress, as is exemplified by their preference for spending the summer in a simple cabin in the forest. One of the most difficult things for a foreigner to understand about the Swedes is the way they manage to combine freedom with conformity. Tomasson (1970, p. 286) suggests it is a 'freedom to' rather than a 'freedom from'. Perhaps it is that Swedes find great security in social solidarity, which thus gives them the confidence to go out and do their own thing. If so they may have solved the problem, dating back to Thomas Hobbes, of the balance between the individual and the collective. In sociological terms, the Swedish welfare state may be seen as providing the post-industrial-revolution social solidarity that Durkheim was looking for.

Tomasson (1970, p. 3) further claims that Sweden is the only small industrial society to be self-sufficient. This is not quite true. Sweden is dependent on oil imports for 74 per cent of its total energy consumption. After the 1973 oil crisis the government made available heavy grants for investments in the saving of energy. However, due to the climate, heating alone takes up 43 per cent of consumption; most modern Swedish homes are extremely well-insulated but use flexible and convenient electric convector heating, although there are schemes to use surplus power-station heat in district distribution schemes where practical. Admittedly Sweden is richly endowed with water power for hydroelectric schemes, which produce 80 per cent of the electricity, through a system that is 52 per cent privately owned, but the water is generally distant from the settlements, with the result that the transmission costs are high. In any case the potential has, since the late 1970s, all been developed. Nuclear power was intended to fill the gap currently taken up by oil-fired power stations, for Sweden has no coal (Jones, 1976), but, as in all the advanced industrial nations, this has run into political problems. The *Centerpartiet* (Centre Party), formerly the *Bondeförbundet* (Agrarian Party), took up the issue of environmentalism, gained widespread support even amongst SAP voters and, supported by the Conservatives and Liberals, were the cause of the SAP's only major absence from government since 1932, between 1976 and 1982. The SAP government which came into power in 1982 instituted a policy of phasing out nuclear power, although the last two units in Sweden's nuclear programme were not commissioned until 1985. This is an indication of the unavoidable links between economics and politics. However, having said all this, and returning to the original point, Sweden has succeeded in remaining extremely independent, if not entirely self-sufficient.

The traditional industries

Sweden has been richly endowed with timber and iron ore, and they have been exploited to effect since medieval times and before, especially in terms of exports and the obtaining of foreign exchange. As mentioned already, in the industrial era the development of plant for timber and iron ore processing gave Sweden not only technological expertise, which could be exploited in many alternative fields, but also, of course, the potential and capacity to generate more export demand.

Agriculture and forestry continue to be important. Through the medium of regional development schemes, sponsored by the government through its devolved Labour Market Board network, they have each been reducing their manning. Agriculture uses only 7 per cent of the workforce, but Sweden aims to be 80 per cent self-sufficient in food for the foreseeable future. The cooperatives continue to be very important for distribution and marketing. Forestry takes up 14.5 per cent of Swedish manufacturing and provides 25 per cent of exports. As an industry it has shown a spectacular growth rate. Steam saw-mills were introduced in 1848, and in 1857 the first pulp-mill went into operation at Trollhätten, followed in 1870 by chemical wood-pulp processing. Between 1894 and 1913 exports were increased ten-fold, establishing the strong Swedish presence in the markets for newsprint, kraft paper and fine writing paper that has lasted to the present time (Scott, 1977). At the turn of the century the industry had already moved into these higher profit areas and, of course, into matches. From Alexander Lagerman's development of the mass production of matches, through the disaster of the Kreuger bankruptcy of 1932, Svenska Tändstick (Swedish Match) has progressed into flooring materials, kitchen fittings, doors and packaging, as well as keeping up production of the original matches. Similarly, other sections of the industry have moved into more profitable areas like furniture, where Scandinavian design can be used to good effect.

Iron and steel are, equally, stalwarts of the Swedish industrial scene and have provided a solid background to the country's development in engineering and technology over the years. They are based upon vast deposits of rich ore in the north of the country, allowing for all types and qualities of metal to be produced. The Sandvik company, which manufactures high-quality steel for instance, has a long-standing reputation for exports, nearly 90 per cent of its production on average going overseas. It is currently Sweden's seventh biggest exporter, but is marginally surpassed by the high-grade ore exports of the mining group SSAB. The Gränges company is the second largest mining group after SSAB and it has concentrated on heavy steel, particularly for the shipbuilding industry.

As in all the European and North American countries, shipbuilding has declined greatly and in Sweden is now mostly concentrated into the state-owned Svenska Varv AB group, which is now quite modest in comparison to the previous proportions of the industry. This state-owned rump of Swedish shipbuilding continues to close yards, as in the case of the one at Uddevalla in 1985–6. Here half the community lost their jobs in a yard which was one of the most up-to-date in the world, hitherto backed by enormous investment. In the standard pattern for declining shipbuilding industries everywhere, the government put in a regional development corporation to attract alternative employment. What is uniquely Swedish about the case is that the unions did not resist the shutdown but involved themselves in it to ensure that the best deal could be wrung out of the government. A new managing director, Leif Molinder, was brought in, with the belief that you cannot compete with the yards in Korea and Japan, and, at the same time, with a record of having previously closed down the Landskrona shipyard with only 1 per cent of the labour force experiencing long-term difficulties. Perhaps the best news was that Volvo, Sweden's most successful company, would open a new plant in the Uddevalla area. Meanwhile Svenska Varv remains Sweden's biggest loss-making company!

Under the guidance of the electrical group, Electrolux, Gränges, the steel supplier, has by comparison survived quite well considering that the decline of Sweden's shipbuilding industry has been as spectacular as the growth in other sectors. In 1971 Sweden was second only to Japan as a shipbuilding country. The Kockums Company at Malmö alone employed 50,000 people in eight yards, producing supertankers on a flow-line production principle, and in a further four yards, producing specialised ships. These were some of the most up-to-date yards in the world. There was a policy of constant renewal and the equivalent of £220 per annum per employee was spent on research and development, including 35 per cent from government grants (Jones, 1976, p. 12).

The interesting point is that the decline has been managed very well, both from the government point of view, in terms of labour mobility and re-training, and from the company point of view, in terms of restructuring. Soon after regaining power in 1982 the SAP government announced that it was to phase out subsidies and re-structure the state-owned industries. Earlier than this Sweden had, in fact, accepted as mistakes both the taxing of the efficient to support the inefficient and the use of state investment to underwrite jobs. By the application of concessions on high company taxation, the profitable are now encouraged to re-invest through the use of investment funds, to be described in Chapter 7.

Despite all this, Svenska Varv, or Swedyards as their advertising calls them, continue to turn in a good export performance. Sweden and the other Scandinavian countries, with their network of vehicle ferries, were amongst the pioneers of roll-on, roll-off vessels, now a bread and butter line with the demise of the super-tanker and bulk-carrier. However Svenska Varv have used their collective expertise to move into not only what has become the standard alternative, oil rigs, but also, and more innovatively, into high-technology thermally-efficient power station systems and into a range of comparable fields.

The central role of rationality

What emerges from any consideration of the development of Sweden is a strong impression of the commitment to secular rationality. A Weberian view, linking the 'spirit of capitalism' and associated scientific and technological advancement with the 'protestant ethic', would associate this with the early establishment of the Lutheran Church as the universal state church in Sweden. This must in turn be linked with the characteristic of the Swedes, expressed previously, to put less emphasis on the individual whilst producing a secure social structure that enables the individual to go out and do things. Swedes do not like to see themselves set above others – it is something they shrink away from; yet they retain a tremendous pride in their country and this is a strong feature of the Swedish educational system and other agencies of socialisation. Internationalist Swedes have not lost their almost Germanic image of the fatherland.

Concentration

The degree of concentration of Swedish industry increased markedly during the period 1942 to 1960 and the process further accelerated during the 1960s. Swedish firms tend to be small on the whole and so this concentration was amongst the larger companies. During the 1960s ASEA employed the most people – about 29,000 and SKF, the ball-bearing manufacturer, had the largest turnover, although it was only 3 per cent of that of General Motors. In 1964 thirty-seven companies had more than 5,000 employees. As in other capitalist industrial nations, it is small groups of shareholders who exercise the power of decision during such processes of concentration and a large shareholder is not always an individual. In fact ownership in Sweden is more concentrated than it is in America or Britain, although the largest firms are not nearly so large. The relations between small shareholders and total holdings are not dissimilar, and so it is board meetings rather than shareholders' meetings that make decisions about unsatisfactory management, mergers, take-overs, etc. (Commission on Industrial and Economic Concentration, 1976).

By comparison with the figures quoted above for the 1960s, today Volvo employs the most people in Sweden, 51,700, plus a further 17,000 abroad; Electrolux employs 89,500 in total, most of whom are abroad. ASEA, the former leader, now employs something in excess of 37,000 people. Volvo also now has the highest turnover, 87 billion krona in 1984, whilst SKF has moved down to fifth position, with nearly 18 billion krona. Volvo's turnover is about 16 per cent of that of General Motors, which is a startling progression from SKF's 3 per cent proportion of the 1960s!

Industry and nationalism in Sweden

Lindbeck (1975) throws some interesting light on the relationship between public and private finance in the development of Swedish industry. The way in which many sources of finance have been exclusively channelled towards Swedish industry, particularly in the sector of new technology, must be seen as a manifestation of Swedish nationalism. It is a means by which nationalism and industrial development have been very usefully combined.

Although the public sector is responsible for only about 15 per cent of the national output of Sweden, and in manufacturing only 5 per cent, it has taken up a growing proportion of the demand side – 15 per cent of GNP in 1939, 17 per cent in 1945, 20 per cent by 1950 and 30 per cent in the 1970s (Adler-Karlsson, 1967). More startling is the fact that, whereas in 1950 only about 25 per cent of the national income (GNP) went to the state, the figure is now between 50 and 60 per cent. Yet the state owns only 6 per cent of Swedish industry, with 2 per cent of that actually in the hands of large municipalities; 90 per cent is in private hands and the remaining 4 per cent is taken up by the cooperatives. The state owns:

SJ – Statens Järnväger (Swedish Railways)
Televerket (the telephone system)
Postverket (the postal services)
Some electricity production
Systembolaget (the state liquor stores)
The LKAB iron ore mines
20 per cent of the northern forest
Svenka Varv (the Swedyards shipbuilding group)

All of these have small administrative structures by comparison with nationalised industries elsewhere. They are made to compete on the open market and are expected to make a profit. In 1984, in fact, the Postverket (postal services) and Televerket (telephones) were the second and third most profitable enterprises in Sweden, respectively.

The state pension fund has become in Sweden, as pension funds have elsewhere, a prime source of industrial finance, but, as with other aspects, the feature of the Swedish case is the rate of growth. In 1950 pension funds represented only 1 per cent of the credit supply, but by 1970 the figure was 40 per cent and the progression continues, despite the economic vicissitudes of the 1970s and 1980s.

Against the background of this brief introduction to industry and technology in Sweden, we will move in the next chapter to a characterisation of Swedish management, then to a discussion of the relationship between management and society, and then come full circle by turning the spotlight on the manufacturing function.

3 The character of Swedish management

One way to begin the characterisation of management in any society is to see where the managers have 'come from', especially in an educational sense. This will give a certain kind of portrait of the managers as one of the society's élite groups; it may also give clues as to the standing of management as an occupation and suggest the things that matter in the eyes of those involved.

In discussing the relations between society and management in Sweden in the next chapter, an opening argument will be that Sweden is marked by what one might call low differentiation; that is to say, people, groups, classes, sexes even, are less apart, less marked off from each other than in many other western societies. This idea is immediately relevant to an examination of the educational backgrounds of managers in Sweden. In comparable British surveys it is natural to categorise managers according to the type of secondary school they attended, and to address such questions as the advantage conferred by a public school education, or the connection between attendance at different secondary school types and later employment in particular areas of management. A good example of this approach is the last management survey carried out by the British Institute of Management (Melrose-Woodman, 1978). In Swede, however, this is a non-issue.

Education and qualifications

The present educational system in Sweden is comprehensive, as indicated in Chapter 1. At seven everyone goes to a *grundskola*, a primary or basic school, and is educated there until the age of sixteen. At sixteen it is possible to leave full-time education and start work, but only a minority do this (about 20 per cent was the figure suggested to us in discussions with Swedish academics). The other 80 per cent or so go to a *gymnasium*. The *gymnasium* offers a variety of courses. Some, differentiated by subject or subject group, lead to the *studentexamen*, the Swedish equivalent of A levels in England, and thence to admission to a university or technical university. Another set of courses lead to a more vocationally-orientated qualification, roughly equivalent to the old Higher National Certificate in Britain; for engineers, for example, such a course leads to the qualification of *gymnasiumingenjör*, for students of economics to that of *gymnasiumekonom*. A third set of courses at the *gymnasium* lead to lower-level vocational qualifications.

The *gymnasium* is the only type of (state) secondary school, and pretty well everyone who continues their full-time education beyond the age of sixteen goes to it. It would be an exaggeration to say there are no private schools in Sweden, but they are few and far between and there are no establishments which equate with the English public schools in terms of standing or exclusiveness.

In the Swedish case there is no real differentiation in terms of the type of secondary school attended, and thus no scope for invidious comparisons! There is also an element of socialist egalitarianism about the system of admission to university in Sweden. University admission is centralised; the *Universitet och Hogskoler Ambetet* (UHA) is the Swedish equivalent of the Universities Central Council on Admissions in Britain (UHA = UCCA), but the UHA does not only respond to nineteen year old *gymnasium* applicants with a full *studentexamen*, even if these are the majority. There are thus several ways of gaining a university place in Sweden.

First, most applicants – somewhere around three quarters – do come direct from the *gymnasium* and do have a full *studentexam*. This exam is graded from 5 to 1, 5 being the highest grade. Whether or not the student of this type gains a place depends on the mix of grades and choice (where does he want to go and what does he want to study). Second there are different arrangements for students who are over twenty-five and who have been at work for four years or more. This group are also required to have a full *studentexam* and to have done, at the *gymnasium*, subjects relevant to the intended university course (e.g. biology for medicine), but they can be given two points (on the 5–1 scale) for their age and work experience. Thus in practice, and in plain English, they can get in with lower A level grades. Third, there is another entry category for people over twenty-five with four years or more work experience who lack the *studentexamen*, but who do have some *gymnasium* study behind them, including the mandatory two years of English. This group are not only allowed up to two points on the 5–1 scale for their work experience; they also have the option of taking the *hogskolapruvet*, a 7-hour aptitude test, which may yield up to two more points.

Furthermore, they can take this aptitude test repeatedly in the interests of getting a top score.

The following generalisations about the educational background and qualifications of Swedish managers are based mainly on the managers we have interviewed and, perhaps more importantly, on what they and others in a position to know described as typical qualification sets for types or levels of management. One could précis the discussions by saying that, in the matter of qualifications, Swedish management conforms to the German rather than the British model (Lawrence, 1980); that is to say, qualification levels appear to be generally higher than in Britain and there is a heavy patterning as to subjects studied.

Take the question of level of qualifications. All the Swedish managers we interviewed, and all those whose qualifications were described to us (a standard tactic was to ask a manager to fill in the qualifications of equal rank colleagues or of those reporting to him), were university graduates or had the *gymnasiumingenjör* or *gymnasiumekonom* qualifications. There were even a number of cases of double degrees. On the subject of the level and range of qualifications there appear, however, to be two points of contrast with Germany, despite the broad similarity.

The first difference is found at the bottom of the system and relates to apprenticeships. In Germany it is common for a manager with the second-level qualification, corresponding to the Higher National Certificate/Higher National Diploma level in Britain or the *gymnasiumekonom/ingenjör* level in Sweden, to have completed an apprenticeship. Indeed, until around 1970 in West Germany a completed apprenticeship was a prerequisite for the courses leading to this qualification (Hutton, Lawrence and Smith, 1977). It is also not uncommon for engineering graduates in Germany to have done an apprenticeship at an earlier stage. There seemed to be very little of this trend in Sweden, the only exceptions being one or two production managers who held an engineering qualification not so far mentioned, that of *institutetsingenjör*. By level the *institutetsingenjör* approximates to the *gymnasiumingenjör*; that is, it is a non-graduate qualification. It is an old-fashioned and part-time alternative to the *gymnasiumingenjör*; to put it in British terms, the *institutetsingenjör* approximates to the Higher National Certificate rather than the Higher National Diploma.

The second point of contrast with Germany is the relative absence of managers with a doctor's degree. Only one of the interviewed managers had a PhD, there were no references to the doctor's degree as a possible or likely manager qualification, and none were spotted on organisation charts. In other words, Sweden resembles Britain in this respect. It is possible that it is different in the chemical industry in Sweden, of which we do not have first-hand knowledge; in West Germany the chemical industry is remarkable for the high concentration of PhDs.

When it comes to the content of qualifications – to the subjects studied – Sweden is just like West Germany. The qualifications of Swedish managers are overwhelmingly in three subjects – engineering, economics and law, and in that order of frequency. Again the chemical industry should be excluded from this generalisation, but otherwise the pattern is remarkably consistent.

All the production managers and managers in the other technical functions had engineering qualifications, whether that of *gymnasiumingenjör* or *institutetsingenjör* described above, or more often the qualification of *civilingenjör* (university degree in engineering). Commercial managers were generally described as having qualifications in economics, again either that of *gymnasiumekonom* described earlier, or *civilekonom* (university degree in economics). Personnel managers are a 'mixed bunch'; the traditional qualification is a law degree, as in Germany, but many have the economics qualification of *gymnasiumekonom* or *civilekonom*, and from the 1960s onwards there have also been personnel managers with sociology degrees obtained at one or two particular university institutes specialising in social science cum social work training.

There seems to have been some change in the pattern of qualifications among heads of companies in Sweden, though perhaps this is not quite the right way to put it. Sweden's strength is in engineering, and most of the big name companies are engineering firms. In the past, and that means the recent past, the great majority had a *civilingenjör* as managing director. Indeed, if one takes all ranks and not just the top, engineers still predominate in Swedish industry. However, at the top, it is generally agreed, there has been a change; starting in the 1960s, there has been a tendency to appoint as managing directors people with a sales or marketing background who, of course, tend to have the *civilekonom* qualification. Today, therefore, most of the larger firms have a *civilekonom* as MD, though there are still some engineers in the top positions, and occasionally lawyers, the most famous being Pehr Gyllenhammer, the head of Volvo.

In some of our interviews with managers and consultants it was suggested that there was a new development, going beyond the move from engineering- to economics-qualified managing directors. This is the current fashion to appoint as managing directors someone who is strongly profit-orientated and alive to business opportunities rather than being simply production- or market-orientated. This point was raised in several of our interviews and it certainly accords with the spirit of the times, but in so far as it is true it refers merely to the top manager's previous assignments and state of mind rather than to his qualifications and training in the narrower sense.

To give some real-life examples, of the first five managing directors we interviewed, three were engineers (*civilingenjör*), one was an economist (*civilekonom*) and the fifth had been educated abroad. Of the three referred to as engineers, all in fact had double degrees, in economics as well as engineering, so that each had the qualifications *civilingenjör* and *civilekonom*. This is rather unusual, but it is also instructive. These three began by enrolling as undergraduates on engineering courses; they then, while still engineering undergraduates, started economics degrees, and eventually graduated in both subjects. As one of them put it: 'When I started I didn't really intend to take the final degree [in economics], but it was so interesting I couldn't give it up.' A production manager we interviewed also had this double qualification – an engineering degree at the start of his career, and an economics degree done on the side later on. When we suggested that this (the economics degree while doing a full-time job) must have been hard work, the idea was dismissed with the observation that the economics course was very easy for an in-service manager who could see the relevance and application of it all. This is Sweden at its best.

Notwithstanding all that is said at various points in this book about egalitarianism and lack of differentiation in Swedish society, there are some informal status gradations in the higher education system in Sweden. Degree courses in engineering are on offer primarily at the technical universities in Sweden. To be more precise, one may do an engineering degree at Lund, where a university and a technical university are on the same site and share some teachers, in the Physics Department at Uppsala University, at the technical universities of Stockholm, Gothenburg and Linköping, and at the University of Lulea in the north-east. However two of these have greater prestige than the others; to give them their Swedish names, in first place is the *Kungliga Tekniska Högskolan* (Royal Technical University) in Stockholm, and a close second is *Chalmers Tekniska Högskolan* in Gothenburg. Both were founded in the second quarter of the nineteenth century, and are immensely prestigious.

When it comes to the economics degree, the *civilekonom*, there is a similar ordering of institutions, according to prestige. Originally the qualification of *civilekonom* was only awarded by the specialist Handelshogskolan in Stockholm, founded shortly after the turn of the century; later a comparable *Handelshögskolan* was founded in the second city of Gothenburg and this also awards the *civilekonom*. These two are probably pre-eminent. The courses at these two establishments, by inference from the textbooks used, appear to be halfway between a conventional economics course and a business course.

The board of directors

Moving next to the question of control and direction, Swedish companies have a single board of directors as in Britain and France, not two-tier boards as in West Germany. In Sweden this board is called the *styrelse*. The board includes, of course, the managing director, called in Swedish the *verkställande direktor* (VD = MD), and, since a law of 1972 described in more detail in Chapter 6, there are also two trade union representatives on the board. These latter are locally elected employees of the company, not outside union officials. The other members of the board are generally non-executive directors in Anglo-American parlance; they are not, that is, senior managers of the firm concerned, but outsiders.

Although the legal requirement is only for a single board of directors, it seems that companies often form a lower level executive committee, usually called a *ledningsgrupp*, chaired by the VD. This compensates for the fact that the *styrelse* is largely non-executive.

Usually the VD is the only member of the top management team to sit on the *styrelse*, and in this he contrasts with the typical British MD who will often have other of his senior managers on the board. This must enhance the 'loneliness of power' for the Swedish VD – a point that was raised by several interviewees in discussing Anglo–Swedish differences.

The two trade union members of the *styrelse* seem to be generally accepted, and in some cases positively welcomed. In their favour it was claimed they could be used as a sounding board and information channel, and one board member spoke of the novelty appeal enjoyed by trade union representatives in the boardroom. It was often suggested that these representatives were more influenced than influencing, and that they did not affect the content of decisions very much. It was sometimes said that they slowed up proceedings by asking awkward questions and by demanding the preparation or provision of factual data. The extended form of this complaint is the not-uncommon allegation that the trade union representatives slow down decision making and cause (especially unpalatable) decisions to be postponed.

Most of the non-executive directors on these boards are full-time managers in other companies, usually financed by the same bank, an arrangement that will be described in more detail in the next chapter. Thus these non-executive directors actually have considerable managerial-business experience, though this fact is perhaps masked by the conventional Anglo–American designation of 'non-executive'.

The chairmanship of the *styrelse* is very unlikely to be vested in the VD, another point of contrast with Britain, where a 'managing director and chairman of the board' set-up is not uncommon. In Sweden the chairman is usually the representative of the dominant shareholder block or, in the case of family firms, the head of the clan.

The overall view most often expressed about the *styrelse* is that it is not really all that important; the *styrelse* is not expected to run the company in a way a German *Vorstand* does (Lawrence, 1980) and a British board may. It is rather an intermittent quasi-ceremonial review body, with day-to-day execution being handled by a *ledningsgrupp*.

Life at the top

The discussions we had with managing directors in Sweden were instructive in several ways. As has been suggested already, some of them are dazzlingly well-qualified, and average qualification levels are substantial. Another circumstantial fact worth recording is the ease with which interviews with managing directors were obtained, and the relaxed and unpretentious nature of the exchanges which followed.

These discussions with Swedish managing directors, taken together and generalised, yield a number of positive and connected impressions. The strongest of these is their extreme export-mindedness – this is the personal aspect of the corporate phenomenon described in the last chapter. Most of the companies visited had an enormous export stake, both by volume and by proportion of output sold abroad. It also appeared that there is a sense in which successful exporting is 'all in the mind' – exporting happens because people believe in it and do the things consequent on that belief.

Statements such as 'We think of Scandinavia rather than just Sweden as our home market' and 'Western Europe is our traditional domestic market but now we are doing more business in Asia' abounded in these discussions.

A second impression is one that might be thought of as corresponding to the first impression – a high degree of product-mindedness. The managers in most cases showed knowledge and understanding of the products and interest in their functioning and application, in how they were derived and in what would happen next. This feature was not as marked as in Germany, but it was more in evidence than in the UK (Lawrence, 1977/8).

A third impression is of a persistent search for new markets or business opportunities. Whatever markets and outlets the companies had, they did not seem to be resting on their laurels. Not only was there all the usual enthusiasm for selling in North America, made more piquant in this case by the American–Swedish population ratio; there were also stirring accounts of sales missions in Eastern Europe, successful counterpart deals and joint ventures with communist countries, and new third world markets. Simply thinking about the size of, say, the population of Indonesia is enough to make a Swedish manager salivate.

Associated with the Swedish manager's export-mindedness and search for new markets is an enlightened interest in new applications – not only new products, but new uses for existing products, modified if necessary, or new applications for existing systems or competences. As one pragmatist put it, 'It's a whole lot cheaper than developing totally new products.' To give an example of the lateral expansion of competence, one of the companies had been set up to develop and produce identity cards for banks and the post office. From this rather narrowly conceived beginning it had developed into a world leader in security documentation and accessing; indeed this company is likely to be the future manufacturer of British passports!

Perhaps an overall way of expressing these positive impressions is to say that these top managers knew what they were doing; not in the simple sense of being resolute rather than indecisive, but in the broader sense of having ambitions and objectives and a set of means in view for their realisation. They would talk about what had seemed to be wrong to them when they took over top jobs, and what measures they adopted to get things better; or they would analyse the (largely unfavourable) contemporary climate and point to openings to be exploited or means for coping. Even those who threw up their hands and described their work as all fire-fighting and daily struggle would still talk about policies and objectives.

None of the managers were especially forthcoming on problems or difficulties, though this may be an expression of Swedish reserve rather than reality. What was said in this connection was not marked by any strong patterns. Probably the two things mentioned most often were the world economic situation – fiercer competition, absence of economic growth, need for cost reductions, and so on – and the material rewards–motivation nexus discussed in the next chapter.

Decision making

Against this background of the impressive quality and stance of top managers in Sweden, it has to be admitted that there is a question mark about decision-making in Swedish companies. Among the people we interviewed there was a rough agreement that decision-making tends to be slow in Sweden. This is particularly a criticism expressed by outsiders such as consultants and others passing judgment on the quality of Swedish management. Three reasons were suggested for this, and a fourth is deducible.

The most obvious cause is the effect of the co-determination system in general, and the *förhandlingsrätt* (right to negotiate) in particular, this system being described in detail in Chapter 6. To this one might add that one manifestation of Swedish perfectionism is the search for the perfect compromise!

Another cause follows from Swedish egalitarianism, in that egalitarianism tends to value everyone's commitment and consent equally. Thus, according to both Swedish managers themselves and others commenting on their *modus operandi*, decision making in Sweden is naturally participative, like a less exaggerated example of Japanese corporate decision-making. It is therefore normal for a Swedish manager to consult his subordinates, and not just to consult them cosmetically.

A third argument, and in a sense an alternative explanation, is entirely critical. Some people we talked to suggested that Swedes are naturally timid, scared of the decision-making limelight and terrified of being thought to act *ultra vires*. If there is one thing that will worry a Swede it is the idea that people will think he is setting himself above them and 'acting uppity'. Participative (and slow) decision-making is thus a response to this latent anxiety, almost a way of covering oneself.

It is, of course, quite possible that both of the last explanations are true, and that Swedes 'participate' for both the right and the wrong reasons. It is also the case that even if the less flattering interpretation is true, it may still have desirable results; that is, those who have 'participated' may well be flattered, will make a valuable contribution, will display the Hawthorne effect and will feel bound to the resultant decision. All this will be good for solidarity and implementation, whatever the cause.

No one we talked to actually stated the fourth point, but it is implicit in some of the testimonies. Put simply, this states that government is more omnipresent, and more intrusive, in Sweden than, say, in the UK (Huntsford, 1971). From the viewpoint of any given company, what the state ordains and requires is likely to set parameters within which that company must operate, more so than in, say, Britain or the USA. Furthermore, the state does not simply require; as was shown in Chapter 1, it consults and collects data before it takes decisions, and during this stage positions will emerge, tendencies will be articulated, and there will be a 'fluid phase' until issues get firmed-up.

All this means that Swedish companies have an interest in effecting the circumstances and climate in which business is conducted, which in turn means lobbying, tapping, and pressing government. Like all negotiating operations, this takes time and adds an element of slowness to the decision process. The point may sound a bit airy fairy, so let us offer one example. Suppose the Swedish government, right-thinking and environmentally conscious, should decide to ban beer cans! It is not inconceivable; the Danish government has already done it. If this should come to pass in Sweden it will effectively ban imports 'at a stroke'. It would also more than compensate for the government's last intervention, the banning of *mellanöl* (medium strength beer) obliging the breweries to substitute (weaker) class II beer, which has not sold so well.

We have kept this introduction to Swedish management deliberately short, and concentrated on a few features – the educational background of Swedish management, the constitution of the board of directors, the disposition of top management, and the character of the decision process – with some signposts forwards and backwards to related discussions in other chapters.

Stock-taking

It was suggested at the outset that the educational background of a country's managers may be indicative of the standing of management as an occupation. It certainly is in the case of Swedish managers, and in several ways. First, the educational system itself is a testimony to Swedish egalitarianism, not just in the sense of being comprehensive but also in the arrangements for university entry. Thus Swedish managers are socialised in structured egalitarianism via the medium of this system. Second, the level of qualifications of Swedish management indicates the high standing of industry in that country – this is one of the themes of the book, and another substantiation of the claim will be offered in the next chapter. Third, the patterning of the content of the qualifications of Swedish managers tells us not just that there is a Swedish–German resemblance, but that it is specialist rather than generalist. Note here the contrast with the USA, whose managers believe they can 'manage anything', or with the typical British manager who is proud to count himself 'a bit of an all-rounder'. The Swedish subject patterning, on the other hand, tells us there is a different Swedish view: that qualified engineers are the people for management posts in production and technical functions; that people who intend to make a career in the commercial functions will take economics qualifications at college; that law is appropriate for personnel management and some general positions; that the up-to-date personnel manager will be qualified in social science; and so on. This represents a difference of orientation, a divergence from the Anglo–American view.

Firstly, in this connection, the dominance of engineers in Swedish management is significant. Swedish language and culture does not, like Anglo-Saxon, divide the world of knowledge and ideas into 'arts' and 'science', thereby implicitly relegating engineering to the hybrid, derogatory status of 'applied science'. Swedish thinking, like German, distinguishes rather between all formal knowledge, whether arts or science, as art, in the sense of its artifacts or performance, and what they call *teknik*, which is the knowledge and skills relevant to manufacturing. It is in line with this that Swedish companies typically exhibit a distinct *teknik*-ethos, in the sense of a predominance of engineers, a higher status enjoyed by the technical functions and a greater concern for design and production.

The Swedish board of directors, and in particular the way in which non-executive members are recruited, are pointers to particular features of business life in Sweden – the overlapping nature of the business élite and the distinctive role of the three major banks. This we will put into context in the next chapter. The successful integration of trade union representatives on to boards of directors is a testimony to Sweden's remarkable ability to make co-determination work. At the same time there is a price to be paid for making it work, a part of which is revealed in terms of the constraints this co-determination makes on management decision-making. A full account of the co-determination system occurs in Chapter 6; this chapter has merely put down some empirical markers in order to give the later discussion more meaning. The references in this chapter to the way government impinges on business life in Sweden is also only the 'tip of the iceberg', in the sense that an underlying theme of this book is that government in Sweden is important. Government in that country has been more formative and more directive in the last 50 years than governments in most western countries; it has aspired to more and accomplished more. Sweden's distinctiveness owes more to government and less to native individualism than in most countries.

Finally the points made in this discussion of the character of top managers in Sweden have a more than individual significance. The tenacity of Swedish managers' export-mindedness, of their product consciousness and of their commitment to business opportunity are at the very heart of Swedish industrial strength.

The next chapter will take this characterisation of Swedish management further, while blending in the theme of the relationship between management and society.

4 Management and society

The overall purpose of this chapter is to look at the connections between management and society in Sweden. To begin with it may therefore be helpful to 'block in' some pictures of Swedish society and the business context. At various points in this book tribute is paid to the high-minded internationalism of Sweden, and rightly so. But for the moment we will look at the other and neglected side of the coin – nationalism.

Nationalism in Sweden

There is a tendency for some small (by population) rich countries to be cultural client states, to be dominated or characterised by larger neighbours. In this vein we have an Anglicised Australia, an Americanised Canada, Belgium as a Franco–Dutch hybrid, and Switzerland as a scenic extension of Bavaria. But Sweden is itself; it is the biggest and most influential of the Scandinavian states, and the dominant member of the Nordic Union. Although Norway, thanks to its oil, is coming to rival Sweden in the GNP-per-capita stakes ('baby brother is trying to become big brother', as one Swede put it to us), Sweden still has the largest population and land area, and certainly better internal communications (it is one of Scandinavia's transport ironies that from Narvik in northern Norway there is a direct train service to Stockholm, but no train connection at all to Oslo). Swedes are also conscious that Norway was once ruled by them (1815–1905) and are resentful of Norway's throwing off of Swedish rule; to make matters worse 'national day' in Norway is 17 May, the anniversary of independence from Sweden. Finland was a Swedish possession for centuries before its conquest by Russia during the Napoleonic Wars, and Swedes still speak approvingly of Finland as being 'like us in many ways'; they clearly regard it as a proper place for Swedes to go to (and feel mildly superior to). Swedes also think of themselves as superior to the Danes, whom they regard as a bit flash and pushy, and Swedes actually speak of 'going to the

Continent', which means going to Denmark (in the first instance). If we emphasise Sweden's nationalism here, it is because it is not generally recognised at all. Sweden's long-standing neutrality and high-minded internationalist stance in foreign affairs do not prepare the visitor to Sweden for manifestations of homely nationalism. To give a simple example of this phenomenon, there are an awful lot of flags in Sweden; boats are festooned with them, and no *residence secondaire* is complete without one. The Swedish flag colours, a very attractive yellow cross on a blue background, also figure endlessly in design and decoration, on everything from T-shirts to hold-alls. To offer another small example, in the fruit and vegetable market in the Hogtorget in Stockholm most produce is labelled as Swedish and the province of origin is also given (the reverse convention prevails among British greengrocers, who only label produce if it is foreign). This symbolises the fairly widespread conviction that if it's Swedish it must be good and the responsible citizen will want to steer clear of foreign rubbish.

Swedish economic life is both internationalist and insular at the same time. On the one hand there is the tremendous commitment to exporting, described in the last two chapters; the typical Swedish company has works in other countries, and these will be real production facilities, not just sales outlets. English-speaking ability is near universal among Swedish managers. It is much more common for Swedish managers to have worked abroad, as opposed to having made foreign business trips, than, say, their British or West German colleagues. It is also clear that Swedes benefit from their socialist-neutral image in business dealings in some other parts of the world; it is regarded as an advantage in eastern Europe and a distinct advantage in the Third World. On the other hand, in Sweden itself a foreigner is struck by the relative absence of non-Swedish elements; for example, there are no foreign banks in Sweden by law, though one is assured that they may trade there using a Swedish bank as an intermediary. There are relatively few foreign companies by British or German standards; there are, for instance, no Ford or General Motors car factories in Sweden – indeed the only cars made there are Volvo and Saab. Nestlé is a minor presence, trading under the name of Findus; ITT is represented by Standard Radio and Telefon, but is dwarfed by the indigenous telecommunications concern of L.M. Ericsson; there are no British or American cigarette factories (cf. West Germany); and most Swedes need to have a good think before they can name any Japanese company operating in Sweden.

Swedishness and homeliness

Another feature of Swedish business life is its indigenous homeliness. Since it is not a big country in population terms, everyone knows everyone else at the top.

This small happy family ethos finds expression in the composition of boards of directors, as indicated in the last chapter. The board of a Swedish company is predominantly non-executive in composition; apart from the managing director and mandatory trade union representatives, the members are outsiders, not senior executives of the firm concerned. However, these non-executive directors tend not to be mere status-lending amateurs but senior executives in other major firms, with one of the major banks as a common denominator. So, as one Swedish interviewee jocularly expressed it, 'when you meet the board of a Swedish company you will find the fellow from SKF, the one from ASEA, the chap from Electrolux, and so on'. In other words, via the mechanism of non-executive directors, there is a high level of interlock among the major Swedish companies, certainly among those in the same 'bank blocks'.

On the subject of these bank blocks there are some differences of opinion. If one asks Swedes which groups of companies are associated with which banks, i.e. which companies form the different blocks, the answers are usually slightly different – it is like asking Germans to describe the *Abitur* ('A' level) system. However the gist of it is that a substantial group of companies, including Saab-Scania, L.M. Ericsson and Electrolux, is associated with the Skandinaviska Enskilda Bank; others, of which the most eminent is Volvo, are associated with the Handelsbank; and a third, if lesser, block is associated with the P.K. Bank. The second difference of opinion among Swedes relates to the rigidity of the block system. One senior manager suggested that the blocks give companies an unusual degree of financial security and effectively remove the possibility of take-over as the ultimate sanction for inefficiency. In contrast, another interlocutor suggested that this state of affairs is a thing of the past, that takeovers do now occur across bank lines and that 'our stock market is quite like yours'.

Nationalism and the status of industry

So far we have tried to outline the stereotype of Sweden: it is a small country, but it is big in Scandinavia – and conscious of this fact; it is somewhat on the edge of Europe yet it has a distinctive culture; it is both neutral and internationalist but at the same time shows a robust and homely nationalism. Furthermore, Swedish business life is marked by elements of national exclusiveness.

It is possible to go further and link Swedish nationalism to the Swedish view of industrialisation. If one inquires as to the status of industry in Sweden, again this may elicit contradictory answers. In the narrow sense, this question relates to career choices among able and well-qualified people. Where the status of industry is high, management will be the first career choice of the able and ambitious, as in the USA, West Germany or Japan; where it is low, national talent will be drawn rather to the state service or the free professions – the traditional case in Britain. In this narrow sense Swedes disagree as to whether industry or the civil service carry more esteem. However, this formulation misses the main point!

There is no doubt about the standing of industry in Sweden; it is simply the case that civil service employment carries high prestige too, though obviously for different reasons. Thus the broader consideration which surrounds the notion of the status of industry is that of the place of industry and industrialisation in the popular mind. Critics of Britain have claimed that both industry and industrialisation have been near 'dirty words' in the British folk memory. Both Correlli Barnet (1972), and Martin Wiener (1981) have argued that in Britain the rejection of industrialism, with a corresponding attachment to notions of rural bliss and aristocratic values, has played a central role in Britain's decline. The important thing is that there is no echo of this in Sweden; indeed the reverse is the case.

To re-run, in a picturesque way, the content of the first two chapters, in Swedish folk memory the story is something like this. Once upon a time there was a poor and isolated country in northern Europe; then along came industrialisation and everything started to get better; then barely a hundred years later they found themselves just about the richest country in the world. There are few countries which have been so completely transformed by industrialisation. For Sweden the starting date was late, but the finishing point was high, and Swedish national pride is inextricably linked with this achievement.

Differentiation re-visited

In the earlier discussion of the Swedish education system and the educational background of Swedish managers, it was suggested that low differentiation – between individuals, groups, classes and sexes

– is a feature of Swedish Society. It is possible to go further and argue that a number of things follow from this low differentiation, or can be cited as manifestations thereof.

Firstly, Sweden has achieved a high degree of sexual equality. This equality exists as a legal, social and behavioural phenomenon. For a foreigner it is most observable in the deportment of women; they defer less, compromise less, marry later (free legal abortion removes one cause of early marriage), are more likely to work, and have greater claims to an independent (of their husband's) career.

Secondly, although it is possible to designate social classes or status groups by occupation or educational level, class is a weak behavioural construct; that is, it is not easy to identify or classify people by social class – there does not seem to be the range of class-related behavioural and stylistic differences with which one is so familiar in England. Swedish society is not quite a monochrome – something that Swedes themselves claim – but one does have to work harder to 'spot the differences'.

Thirdly, in Sweden there is relatively low differentiation as to net earned income. To say that 'differentials' are lower in Sweden would be true, but this English usage of the word is too narrow. It is not just that wage differences between various skill grades of blue-collar workers, or between production workers and first line supervisors, are narrower; the wage span for the whole occupational structure falls between closer limits than is the case in Britain. Thus the differences between managerial and worker salaries, between the salaries of various managerial grades, between graduate and non-graduate salaries, are all rather less than one is used to in other western European countries.

In this connection it should be remembered that Sweden is not just a rich industrial country, 'like all the others'. As shown in the first chapter, it has had a social democratic regime for the majority of the last fifty years, and all the triumphs of modern Sweden sustain its image and standing. This combination of high GNP per capita plus long-standing socialist government gives the country a different profile in regard to actual observable wealth. Its most obvious manifestation is a steeply progressive personal income tax, such that marginal taxation rates of 70 to 85 per cent are common among middle-class salary earners. The wider phenomenon is that Swedish national wealth shows up in the absence of poverty, in the high minimum incomes, in the statutory care of the unfortunate and disadvantaged, and in the level of welfare benefits. It does not show up in conspicuous consumption among the rich, which is generally frowned upon. Nor does it show up in terms of greater (than in Britain) affluence among the middle class.

Fourthly, there is a strong commitment to egalitarianism. Not only is Swedish society undifferentiated, as suggested here; there is also a widespread feeling that this lack of differentiation is right, that this is the way things should be. Swedish vernacular is replete with expressions of the *en man är lika god som en an* (a man is as good as anyone else) kind. It is bad to act 'uppity', to set yourself apart from others; displays of wealth are frowned upon, and styles tend to be national rather than segmented or stratified. Associated with the egalitarian norm is the norm of accessibility, bureaucrats, politicians and public office holders are expected to be accessible. If you recognise the minister of transport in the airport lounge you can complain to him about the delay. To give an actual example, alcoholic drink is a state monopoly in Sweden, all purchases being made at a chain of government off-licences called a *systembaloget*. When the government decided not to open the *systembolaget* shops on Saturday mornings, it proved a wildly unpopular move. Several people told us that at the time of the controversy they had rung up the relevant cabinet minister to voice their views. In Sweden you have to have a good reason for not seeing someone, and putative status differences are not enough. The present study has undoubtedly benefited from this phenomenon, as was suggested in the last chapter; if you want to interview managing directors in Sweden you just call them up and ask them!

Fifthly, it is conceded by many people that Sweden's tradition of neutrality in world affairs is paralleled by a certain avoidance of conflict, a non-aggressive peaceableness at home. Patience, restraint, moderation, emotional control are Swedish virtues. Swedes do not like conflict, confrontation and inter-personal challenge. Problems should be solved by discussions leading to compromise, not by *force majeure*. Stockholm is probably the only European capital in which one can drive across the downtown area in the rush hour without hearing a car horn 'sounded in anger'.

Sixthly, there is a corporate dimension to Swedish society. Individuals join groups, associations and federations; it is a way that one expresses one's adult citizenship and claims one's civic rights. And, of course, the biggest corporation of all is the government in the widest sense, including the civil service and associated bodies. Employment in this government bureaucracy is extensive, and increased throughout the 1970s (Telesis Inc., 1980). Right-wing politicians seeking to strike a Thatcherite pose threaten merely to reduce the *rate of increase* of the bureaucracy.

It is possible to argue that Sweden's blossoming bureaucracy and plethora of corporate organisations is not simply a reflection of the social welfare responsibilities assumed by the state (the common assumption). It can also be argued that it is a reflection of the lack of differentiation which has been the *leitmotiv* of the present chapter. Sweden prefers group values to individual values, and group values naturally find corporate expression.

Some of these themes have a characterising affect on Swedish management. The issue of corporatism is a case in point, as exemplified by the SAF, the Swedish Employers' Federation described in the first chapter. Although most countries have such an organisation, the SAF (Svenska Arbetsgivareföreningen) is unusually well-established. It has a central place in the Swedish industrial relations–pay bargaining arena (see Chapter 6) and is the focus of considerable loyalty from member companies.

SAF gained its strength after 1944, when the massive demand for Swedish manufactured goods, accompanied by a labour shortage, increased the need for employer discipline on pay settlements and poaching. What, however, makes SAF distinctive is that it has a central role in Sweden and evokes a high level of member loyalty. There is a famous and recent case in which Volvo made a pay deal with employees in excess of that ordained by the SAF–LO agreement (about 4 per cent in excess). SAF responded by fining Volvo; Volvo paid the fine, and came back into line. This kind of occurrence is absolutely inconceivable in Britain, where the corresponding organisation, the Confederation of British Industry (CBI), is no more than a loosely structured interest group.

This expression of neutrality, this avoidance of conflict in Swedish society is also relevant as a characterisation of industrial management. Again the point may be expressed in a personal way; in interviewing Swedish managers one is struck repeatedly by their reasonableness, and in some cases by a quality almost of gentleness. Swedish managers are less aggressive, less individualistic and less wilful than their colleagues in Britain and Germany. To this impression should be added a consistent finding from the interviews. Swedish managers, when asked open-ended questions about problems and difficulties, mention conflicts, misunderstandings and aggravation with other functions and departments much less than is the case with their British colleagues. And this applied particularly to production managers. Production managers are a good test case because the production function is central; it has dealings and dependencies with many other functions and is often in conflict with them (Hutton and Lawrence, 1978). It was noticeable that these Swedish production managers were very sparing in their criticisms of other departments – of engineering, design, quality control, sales, maintenance, purchasing and so on. And where criticisms were expressed they tended to be more restrained, and often denoting attempts to see the other person's point of view, so that one encountered remarks like 'Purchasing do find it difficult sometimes' rather than 'purchasing has let us down again', or 'Of course quality control has to have a different set of priorities' rather than 'Quality control are buggering us around as usual.'

In one of the later interviews we discussed this impression with a senior Swedish manager. He expressed the view that Swedes, more than most nationalities, would be reluctant to admit to internal rivalries and conflicts. This may well be so, yet the present interpretation was supported by a Swedish lecturer at a management training establishment who listed for us the things managers attending a series of courses complained of – and this enumeration did not include conflict or difficulties with other departments. Again, during our time in Sweden we also had the good fortune to meet several British expatriates, some with considerable experience in business and management. This lack of aggression cum disposition to reasonableness was a common theme among this group as well. One, a manager with some twenty years experience in Sweden, argued that there is, relatively speaking, a lack of 'politicking' in Swedish companies. There is less inter-personal rivalry, less bucking for promotion at all costs, and less in the way of manoeuvres to advance one's own interests at the expense of someone else. A particular example proferred in this connection was the British trick of setting up a superior so that he discredits himself, in the hope of being promoted to replace him; this, it was said, was pretty well unknown in Sweden.

This aspect of Swedish management has so far been expressed very much in negative terms – avoidance of conflict, relative absence of inter-departmental strife and personal rivalries. However it would also be fair to draw attention to the positive aspect – what might be called the cult of competence. There is in Sweden no amateur point of view; if you don't know, you shut up and let those who do know tell you. In so far as initial contacts in Sweden have a hidden agenda, it is to establish the competence of the various parties, not their relative status.

This cult of competence is one dimension of Swedish egalitarianism. Competence is, at least in theory, something which all can
acquire; as such it is a more acceptable discriminator than some kind
of acquired status. Competence is also very Swedish in another sense.
In the Swedish view, for any challenge, task or problem, there will,
on the whole, be one best way of making it, doing it, solving it or
arranging it. To reach this desirable end point, competence is what one
needs, plus patience and a readiness to compromise where necessary.

The behavioural manifestations of Swedish egalitarianism are
quite striking. One aspect of this is linguistic. The Swedish language
has two words for you, *ni* and *du*. They are respectively the formal
and the intimate forms of address, corresponding to *vous* and *tu* in
French, or more closely to *Sie* and *Du* in German. This said, the *du*
form in Swedish is used almost universally, from juniors to seniors,
from workmates to total strangers at bus stops. The use of the *ni*
form, one Swede avowed, would suggest that the speaker was a high
government official. An expatriate Englishman claimed the *ni* form
was now used only at SAS (Scandanavian Airlines System) check-in
counters.

This egalitarianism of manners is also held to be of relatively
recent origin. As late as the 1950s the Swedes were still being
described as excessively formal and off-puttingly reserved. Furthermore, this egalitarianism is a quality of which Swedes are now
militantly proud, and it has clear implications for management. For
example, egalitarianism should reduce the gulf between 'the two
sides of industry', or, more modestly, between management and
workers. It should facilitate communication inside factories and
favour communication upwards from the shop floor. It should
reduce inter-personal friction between ranks, and be a value to which
all may appeal. And, in fact, Swedes tend to claim that all these things
are true. Egalitarianism and ease of communication between manager and worker was the most frequent response to an open-ended
question about the distinctiveness of Swedish management, and it
was also made a point of comparison in Sweden's favour between
Sweden and other countries, with Britain stigmatised as a hot-bed of
stiff-necked privilege, the USA (occasionally) as pseudo-democratic,
and Germany as hierarchical and authoritarian. As a small aside on
the last point, Swedes seem to hold ferociously hostile stereotypes of
the Germans, somewhat worse than those prevalent among elderly
Englishmen. Perhaps the Swedes need some *alter ego* for differentiation purposes – some other nation as a backdrop to their own shining
egalitarianism.

Mobility and motivation

Some of the features mentioned here – high sex equality, low class-based behavioural differences, and a relatively narrow income distribution reinforced by a highly progressive income tax – are together relevant to a discussion of manager mobility and motivation.

The mobility of managers

Let us take mobility first. Swedish managers are not very keen to be moved (geographically), and are similarly not very keen on promotion which involves moving. It may be helpful here to do a burlesque Anglo–Swedish comparison. When an English manager is moved, the move is typically in the form of promotion; in a rank-and-status-crazy society, that promotion is worth something – more so than in Sweden. The move–promotion will generally be accompanied by a salary increase, and this is worth having too, even after tax. The move may also be accompanied by a new (bigger and better) company car. Furthermore, the mobile manager's progress around Britain will be smoothed by the panoply of company-paid estate agent's and solicitor's fees, bridging loans where necessary, and a relocation allowance. Wives may grumble a bit, but not too much, and even if it is a bit of a bore having to make new friends, there will be material compensations, including spending the relocation allowance – an orgy of soft-furnishings and fitted kitchens.

In Sweden, on the other hand, the manager's wife will probably be a working graduate with a career she will be reluctant to jeopardise or interrupt. And in many cases this will be the end of the matter. Furthermore, the promotion itself will count for less in egalitarian Sweden than in Britain: the accompanying pay rise will be less than it would be in Britain, and will be further reduced in value by a steeper income tax progression; company cars are few and far between in Sweden, and are heavily taxed (fringe benefits in general are scarce by British, let alone American, standards, and are taxed to near worthlessness); and Swedish kitchens are all magnificently fitted anyway (and have so many electric gadgets that it is a wonder the floors in some of these multi-storey flats can support them).

Going to work abroad is a special instance of the problem for Swedish managers. The question of what is owed to the wife is then even more acute since she is very unlikely to be able to work in the foreign country; her career is thus in suspense for the duration of the foreign posting, and may suffer permanent damage. On the other hand there are material benefits in the case of an overseas posting. The pay rise is likely to be more substantial; it will conform to local or international norms, not Swedish ones. It is an established part of Swedish management folklore that the expatriate head of a foreign subsidiary will earn more than the overall chief executive back home in Stockholm or Gothenburg. The expatriate manager will also pay tax at local rather than Swedish rates. And there are further 'corrupting inducements' associated with working abroad, of which the most frequently mentioned is having servants (unthinkable in Sweden, for obvious reasons).

It is also the case that an overseas posting is more common for Swedish managers anyway than for their British counterparts, partly because of the strong export orientation of Swedish industry and partly because so many Swedish companies maintain manufacturing establishments outside Sweden. In fact, only a small minority of all the managers we interviewed had not worked abroad. Thus the possibility of such a posting is something with which the individual must come to terms. One management consultant suggested that although starting salary should not be the subject of too much hard bargaining in the appointment interview, it is quite in order to take a hard line on foreign postings. You should actually say 'I don't expect to have my life turned upside down and be sent to Brazil in a couple of years.' Alternatively, in the unlikely event that you would welcome such a posting, you should certainly say so, because it would be a great selling point. A Swedish MD summed up the ambiguity surrounding foreign postings with the remark 'You've got two problems; the first is getting managers to go abroad, and the second is getting them to come home.'

Motivation and rewards

There is, of course, a wider issue than the Swedish manager's reluctance to move – the more central question of motivation and rewards.

The three key facts relating to this issue have all been mentioned already, but it is probably helpful to restate them together. First, Swedish managers are poorly paid by international standards. They know it, and are frequently voluble on the subject. Second, an income tax system which is more sharply progressive than that in most west European countries reduces further the net income of the Swedish manager. Third, fringe benefits are few, and are invariably taxed. Thus the 'material rewards package' enjoyed by Swedish managers compares unfavourably with that in many western countries.

If one deduces anything from this it must be that there is some lessening of motivation and involvement; this would certainly be the American orthodoxy. It is also fair to say that plenty of Swedish managers, and others such as consultants passing an informed opinion, say that this is indeed the case. However it is possible to go even further and point to particular alleged manifestations of this impoverished motivation.

The first is diminished concern with promotion. It has to be said that not every young Swedish manager wants to get to the top, or at least get as far as he can, but in speaking of their objectives Swedish managers are more likely to express themselves in terms of an equation of work and family satisfactions, without the implication that the former should dominate the latter. Now it may be objected that managers in other countries are not really so overwhelmingly committed to work and advancement, or at least that not many of them are. However, even if this counter-argument is conceded, it is still true that there are other countries which pay lip service to the ambition-drive-achievement syndrome. Sweden does not do this; instead Swedes typically take, according to your prejudices, a more balanced or less involved view of the relationship between a manager and his employing organisation. Certainly several senior managers in Swedish companies referred to the difficulty of getting people to accept promotion.

Second, there is an alleged, and obviously related, tendency to avoid exposed line jobs in management. By line jobs we mean posts where the manager is manifestly accountable for performance, where he often has large numbers of subordinates and where he is generally 'in the thick of things'. Such positions are typically in sales, production and general management. The implicit contrast is with more advisory, more 'sheltered', staff jobs. Indeed, it is noticeable that such line jobs are often staffed by people who appear younger than their opposite numbers in other countries. Popular wisdom is that only the young are ready to accept the challenge (and aggravation) of such positions, in default of adequate financial rewards.

Third, a corresponding tendency is both alleged and, in our view, observable, this being the sideways slide into relatively protected staff jobs. Several times such instances were pointed out and it was clear that individuals were sometimes prepared, in the relative absence of a financial deterrent, to give up increments of power for the prospects of a quieter life. Managerial 'decolonisation' is at least as common as empire building.

There are some further manifestations of impoverished motivation, relating not just to low pay but to wider family values. These are, briefly, a reluctance to work long hours, a disinclination to engage in business travel (especially trips which violate the weekend) and the view that holidays are sacrosanct. It is a standing joke in Sweden that the country closes down in July, when it is impossible to get anything done in the business world (and August is not a great deal better). Another point sometimes mentioned in this context is a lack of enthusiasm for business entertaining, felt to be either an unreasonable demand on the manager's (working) wife or an intrusion on family leisure time. Finally, there is the previously discussed phenomenon of reluctance to move.

In so far as these latter charges are true, it is not necessarily, or only, a reflection of the relatively impoverished material rewards package. Sex equality, the importance attached to family life in general, the Swedes' characteristic enthusiasm for nature, scenery and second houses in the country, are all relevant. All one can say is that the Swedish manager is less likely to be deflected from these alternative leisure-family-equality values by crude financial incentives than are his opposite numbers in other countries.

However, even if we accept American orthodoxy on the importance of a high level of financial reward in order to sustain a high level of motivation, and therefore assume that there is some loss in the Swedish case, it cannot be said that it is all loss. In short, there are some corresponding gains.

First, there may be a gain in what one might call 'purity of motive'. Swedish managers who do move, who accept promotions and who fill exposed line posts are rather less likely to be 'doing it for the money' than their colleagues in other countries. Those who get to the top must want to be there for intrinsic rather than extrinsic reasons. Second, the lower financial incentives defuse somewhat the struggle for promotion; if there is a loss of thrusting dynamism there is the corresponding gain which has already been referred to – less politicking, fewer power struggles, more cooperation between functions and hierarchical levels. Third, there is a certain ritual element, in both Britain and the USA, in moving managers around geographically – it is a habit, a *rite de passage*, a test of the manager's loyalty and a celebration of Anglo–Saxon generalism. However, this nonsense element is likely to figure less in Sweden; if it is difficult to get people to move anyway it is therefore more likely that they will only be asked to do so for serious reasons. Fourth, not only are Swedish managers poorly paid by international standards; so are Swedish engineers – and of course the two categories overlap substantially. This is another way of saying that Swedish engineers are cheap – the second cheapest in Europe (after British engineers). In turn, this should be significant for an advanced industrial economy with a lot of highly-engineered up-market products. After all, it is commonly said that high blue-collar wages in Sweden push up the cost of Swedish manufactures and tend to make them uncompetitive; but if this argument is accepted, then so should the countervailing argument about the cheapness of Swedish engineers.

Standing back

It is always a good move to examine the links between management and society in any country as this often provides clues to interesting differences. Looking at this relationship is an integral part of the characterisation exercise.

This general argument is given a particular thrust in the case of Sweden because there is, in Sweden, a tension between socialism and capitalism. The present chapter has shown how some of this tension is expressed; other dimensions are considered in the later chapters on industrial relations and politics and industry.

The socialism–capitalism tension has one very tangible manifestation which has been indicated here, this being the gap between the reward-and-allocation system developed by a welfare socialist state on the one hand, and the near universal norms relating to the reward and remuneration of managers on the other. This tension has implications for the geographical mobility of managers, for self-selection for management posts, for attitudes to overseas assignments, for promotion and for the readiness to be promoted. Furthermore it is felt to contribute to the reasonable and cooperative ethos of the typical Swedish company.

Side by side with this tension – between the objectives and achievements of a socialist society and the values and operating mode of free-enterprise capitalism – is another odd contradiction, the fascinating mixture of internationalism and nationalism in Sweden. It is unusual for countries to have a commitment to internationalism as strong as that of Sweden's, and the fact that this 'cohabits' with simple folksy nationalism is really remarkable.

A further point of interest is the way that Swedish industry benefits from both these characteristics. Sweden's internationalist stance does offer Swedish companies an *entrée* to eastern European and third world markets, while 'nationalism at home' tends to protect domestic consumer markets. As we have agreed earlier, it is also the case that national pride is fuelled by a sense of industrial achievement, and in turn constructively supports that achievement.

5 Manufacturing in Sweden

There are several reasons for devoting a chapter to the manufacturing or production function. The first is that it affords some interesting contrasts with Britain. The second is that to explore the organisation of production in Swedish companies is to investigate a Swedish strength. The third reason is that the exercise will offer some practical insight into the operation of the co-determination system, alongside the systematic account given in Chapter 6 of industrial relations.

Production and status

Research on the production function in Britain in the late 1970s was largely informed by the idea of the relatively low status of production, and the implications thereof. From this starting point, of the idea of production as a 'Cinderella function', it is possible to go on to construct a rough pecking order for the various management functions – one which in Britain puts marketing and finance at the top and design and production at the bottom. This gives rise to the question 'Is it the same in Sweden?'

In a strict sense it probably is. If one puts these British status relativities to Swedish managers as propositions for comment, and asks if there is some similar approximation in Sweden, they are more likely to assent than deny. But this strict sense is also misleading. Firstly, there is a difference of degree, in Sweden's favour. Such status differences, admitted by most Swedes when pressed, are less marked. Secondly, and more importantly, they are less keenly felt, figure less in Swedish consciousness and are much less likely to be articulated. Thirdly, as suggested in the earlier discussion of the qualifications of top managers, there has been some change in the priorities in the 1970s and 1980s in Sweden, with a swing at first in favour of marketing and then in favour of finance and profit consciousness. The reverse side of the coin is the tremendous emphasis on production in the immediate postwar period, and the corresponding dignity attaching to the design-production-engineering nexus. This sustains the production function in Sweden, and unfortunately there is no equivalent heritage in Britain.

A final consideration on this question of the status of production in Sweden is that line production posts are very exposed. Consequently they tend to attract the relatively young and vigorous (rather than the 'old faithfuls' mentioned in a report on the production function in Britain (Business Graduates Association, 1977)). One reflection of this is the apparently high qualification profile of Swedish production managers, again referred to earlier.

Teknik again

Another characteristic of production managers in Sweden is that their work is viewed as more explicitly technical than is that of their counterparts in, say, the UK. This is signified not only by a higher technical threshold in qualification terms but also by more integration and interchange of personnel between the various technical functions, including production; a fact that comes out when one asks individual production managers in Sweden about the sequence of jobs and assignments they have had.

This again is reflected in the relative absence of complaints by production managers in Sweden about the service received from, or the relationship with, other contingent functions. In contrast, surveys in Britain tend to indicate a fairly high level of dissatisfaction by production managers with these associated functions, and to highlight a recurrent tension between sales and production (Lockyer and Jones, 1980). To give a hard example, there was only one occasion in our series of interviews with Swedish production managers when a criticism of the maintenance function emerged, and this was couched in rather impersonal terms of maintenance being an unsystematic operation.

Problems in production

This is not to suggest that the Swedish production manager leads a problem-free existence, but both the degree and the emphasis may differ from what one is used to in Britain. Certainly the interviews with managers yielded relatively little under these headings. Perhaps the best source on this subject is the testimony of a lecturer running a series of short courses for in-service production managers, and able to tap their cares and grievances in informal discussion. This source suggested that the three problems raised most frequently are:

1 The general problem of motivating people.
2 Management of own time.
3 The search for some system of work organisation and payment which will motivate production workers.

The second issue, that of the management of time, is a universal management problem, restricted neither to Sweden nor to the production function. However the first and third issues relate not only to each other but also to the general question of the material rewards–commitment nexus explored in Chapter 4, where low income differentiation and high taxation, combined with an emphasis on family and leisure values, tend to limit the commitment to work.

In the production area this phenomenon has further ramifications. Perhaps the most obvious is the different place of overtime in the Swedish scheme of things. In Britain, overtime working is almost universally sought by employees as a desirable, nay necessary, income supplement. Indeed, in Britain one may witness discussions between foremen or production managers and potential employees conducted purely in terms of the amount of overtime earnings and of the extent to which overtime can be guaranteed, with basic pay being treated as peripheral. That this state of affairs is not a universal feature of industrial life is illustrated by the situation in West Germany, where higher basic rates and higher productivity render overtime working both less attractive and less often required. Sweden, where taxation renders the financial rewards of overtime working much smaller, represents the far end of the continuum. In Sweden, production managers, seeking to underline their personal influence and the cooperative nature of the workforce, speak of the workers' willingness to perform overtime work in order to oblige the company (although not in the summer!)

Supervision

Another manifestation of the difference between the British and Swedish perception of production concerns the Swedish understanding of the famous 'problem of the first line supervisor'. The Anglo–American version is that the combined effect of the growth of technical specialisms and of union power has been to undermine the foreman's authority (Child, 1975). The presumed result is a denuded supervisory role, low morale among foremen and, in some cases, difficulty in recruiting foremen. In an earlier study in West Germany it became very clear that this state of affairs is not necessarily universal; indeed in that country 'the problem' is very much less in evidence (Fores, Lawrence and Sorge, 1978).

When it comes to Sweden, it is difficult to discuss this problem in its Anglo–Saxon purity because of differing Swedish conditions. It tends to be re-defined by Swedish managers as a problem of relative income, and is thus lost in the malaise of high tax and low differentials. The Swedish version of the problem is therefore 'Who would want to be foreman for so little extra money?'

And there is another twist, which is that trade unionists via the *företagsnämnd* or MBL committee – institutions of co-determination discussed in more detail in Chapter 6 – will affect the selection of foremen (and, according to several interlocutors, the selection of higher production managers too), tending to screen out bad guys, bad unionists, or candidates thought to be too dynamic or uncompromising. Thus it is possible that there are some wishy-washy foremen around in Swedish factories.

Productivity and absenteeism

Productivity is sometimes felt to be a problem in Sweden, and on more than one occasion executives we talked to, with works both in Sweden and in other countries, showed productivity to be higher abroad. The problem is not over-manning, and still less under-modernisation, but a blend of long holidays and high absenteeism. This absenteeism is a distinctively Swedish phenomenon, and needs some unpacking.

The Swedes probably count as the fittest nation on earth, and longevity in Sweden is high. Despite this, though, it is still conceivable that there *is* more absenteeism resulting from minor illness-cum-skiving than is the case in Britain; it is not necessary for a Swedish employee to produce a doctor's certificate until he has been off work for a week, yet sickness benefit is paid from the commencement of indisposure – there is no waiting or qualifying period. Absenteeism resulting from illness, however, would appear to account for roughly only half of all absenteeism, as the figures in Table 5.1 for the two works of one of the companies we visited suggest.

It should be said straight away that this is not a case of stacking the cards with an extreme example; it is generally acknowledged that absenteeism in Sweden runs at about 20 per cent. The point is rather to indicate that there are causes other than illness. These include military service, which in Sweden is a rolling incremental obligation;

Table 5.1 **Absenteeism through illness in two Swedish works**

	Works A %	Works B %
Absent for up to a week through illness	5.6	3.5
Absent for more than a week through illness	5.8	8.5
Total absenteeism including that from other causes	21.8	19.8

people always seem to be going off for three weeks, or whatever, just as in Switzerland. Then employees are allowed to take time off to care for a sick child at home; this is an explicit right in Sweden, not just something that happens in a fudged-up way as in Britain. Furthermore, an employee is allowed a year off to care for a newborn child; it is usually the mother that does this, but it does not have to be, and occasionally men do it. This is called taking *pappaledighet*, and it is jokingly said that for a man the ability to take *pappaledighet* is the acid test of occupational security. Only those whose talents or qualifications are very much in demand, say systems analysts, would risk trying it on. The normal managerial view, incidentally, is that an executive ought not to take *pappaledighet*, and it would damage his career if he did. One also hears of managerial colleagues putting pressure on managers not to take *pappaledighet*, and doing so with the tacit encouragement of the managing director. However the fact remains that in Sweden men do sometimes adopt these caring responsibilities.

Swedes usually suggest, however, that the most important component of these high absenteeism rates is time taken off for study for higher education – this is probably the key element in the non-medical absenteeism in the example in Table 5.1. Works A, in particular, is located in a rural area near the Norwegian border, an area offering little in the way of alternative employment – hence the pull of further education. Employees who take time off for educational purposes do not receive wages from their companies (it is the state which pays them); the company's obligation is rather to release the employee in the first place and to keep his or her job open in the second. Of course it often happens that the employee does not return, having qualified for a better job, but the fact remains that the company concerned has to keep the job open and accept the returning employee where the latter so desires.

Now Swedish production managers claim they are little affected by this high absenteeism rate. Educational leave, for instance, is planned ahead and cover can be arranged. It is only no-notice absenteeism which is disruptive and creates manning problems, and this means primarily medically-determined absenteeism. This judgment of disruption of course only refers to day-to-day operations. On the other hand, the high national rate of absenteeism is pulling down the productivity figures and, other things being equal, increasing unit costs. Absenteeism does not, however, appear to affect Sweden's performance or reputation for punctuality of delivery.

On schedule

There is a widely held belief that British industry is bad at delivery punctuality, at getting goods and orders to customers on time. In the formal sense the evidence for this belief is limited, but what studies there are unfortunately tend to show that the charge is all too true (New, 1976).

In particular, there is an especially interesting study of industrial buying and selling in five countries – Britain, France, West Germany, Italy and Sweden (Turnbull and Cunningham, 1981). Buyers and sellers in all the countries were asked to rate companies both in their own country and in all the others on a number of dimensions relevant to industrial buying and selling. Thus, for instance, the study produced data on the qualifications of salesmen, both technical and commercial, from companies in the five countries; it graded the countries in terms of the willingness of companies to undertake additional design work for customers, to make modifications to existing products, or to enter into general technical cooperation with their customers; it enabled the countries to be graded as to the quality and reliability of their products, and showed which countries sought to compete by price (Britain and Italy) and which by product excellence (Germany and Sweden).

The study also took a discriminating look at the question of delivery performance. The first comparison related to manufacturing lead times, i.e. how long companies said they needed to make something. The second comparison was a direct measure of delivery performance; did the companies concerned actually deliver on time? The third comparison looked at the countries in respect of the tendency of their companies to inform customers, in good time, if orders were running late.

Britain came out bottom on all three counts. To burlesque it a little, the British companies wanted longer than anyone else to make products; they then did not finish on time, and compounded the problem by not warning their customers until too late! Incidentally, much of the material in Turnbull and Cunningham's study is presented in a way that enables one to see which countries are giving 'good and bad' marks to which, and what typically emerges from these analyses is that the severest critics of Britain are the British themselves. At the other end of the scale were two 'hero-countries' with respect to delivery performance – West Germany and Sweden. In fact, of the two, Sweden was just ahead.

Whenever the opportunity arose in our own study in Sweden we questioned production and other managers about the company record on delivery performance, and the responses were entirely in line with the Turnbull and Cunningham survey results (1981); that is to say, managers cited low delivery failure rates, the highest being 18–20 per cent of all orders. This shows Britain up in a very unfavourable light, taking as the British base-line the survey by Colin New (1976). Another feature of the Swedish response to our question of delivery punctuality was to take relatively minor failures seriously and agonise over them, German style. On one occasion a production manager, questioned on the point, said that the delivery performance on the majority of orders was reasonable, but on the minority, where the production department had been asked to undercut the stated lead-time, the record was poor. He then paused and said that perhaps, as the senior production manager, he had given a somewhat rosy picture of the delivery performance and called in a marketing manager to give his view. The latter described the performance for the majority of orders as 100 per cent, and put the record on fast orders, where lead-times had to be undercut, at 50 per cent.

Maintenance and investment

A conceivably related factor to this low failure rate is that none of the interviewed production managers mentioned machine breakdowns as a problem, and on endless tours of Swedish factories we did not actually see any broken-down machines undergoing repairs. This in turn relates not only to the technical mentality referred to at the beginning of this chapter but also to investment. The majority of the companies we visited said that they had investment programmes, even during the relatively lean years of the 1980s. There seemed to be a double pattern; firms doing well said they were investing in order to stay on top, and firms doing badly spoke of investing in order to do better next time round.

Swedish production managers' objectives

It is possible to raise the more general questions of 'What are production managers in Sweden aiming at? What are their current priorities and middle-term objectives?'

The impression gained in the interviews is that there is a general pattern whose key is decentralisation. One of the consultants interviewed confirmed that the idea of decentralisation in manufacturing has been a fashion (and fetish) in Swedish industry in the last few years. The basic idea is that a manufacturing entity is broken down into a number of sub-units, termed, for instance, 'product workshops', and that these become semi-independent and responsible for costs, quality and output. Organisationally, these product workshops will have their own production control, production engineering, quality control and perhaps purchasing support.

This leads to a second, and associated, idea which is the delegation of quality control/inspection to production workers, even if some extrinsic inspection department carries out later, and perhaps random, checks. This inspection-in-production or in-progress-inspection idea came up in many of the works we visited; in some, Japanese-style quality circles had also been established, and these, with their deliberate inclusion of operators, are a further manifestation of the same phenomenon.

Another objective is the attempt to reduce work-in-progress; that is, to reduce the number of jobs that are part-finished at any point in time – work-in-progress represents tied-up money and materials. This is obviously an aspect of the new profit-mindedness and cost consciousness referred to earlier. One aspect of this objective, mentioned several times in our interviews, is the attempt to reduce work-in-progress by a better integration of manufacturing lines. In an example given at one of the factories visited, the final product was put together from some five sub-assemblies, each of which was manufactured on its own 'feeder line'. Under the old regime these five lines had produced sub-assemblies at uneven rates; the sub-assemblies had then gone into store in uneven numbers, to be taken out and assembled later. The new regime aimed at integrating the output of the five feeder lines and making the necessary tooling and manning changes so that they would produce the sub-assemblies, in phase, and for immediate final assembly.

There is another feature observed which fits in with this decentralising–streamlining movement, though it is quite possible that it existed before. This concerns the organisation of the purchasing operation. In Britain the purchasing function is enjoying a rise in status and importance. This, of course, is connected with the recessionary period of the early 1980s which put a premium on cost-cutting; the easiest way of reducing the price of the final product is to reduce the cost of raw materials and bought-out parts, and this in turn enhances the importance of buyers, i.e. those responsible for doing the purchasing. Thanks to a British Institute of Management survey, we also know that the typical purchasing department in British industry is organisationally independent; that is to say, it is not subordinate to a higher-level production manager or attached to finance or sales, though such minority arrangements do occur (Farrington and Woodmansey, 1980). This appears to give a point of contrast with Sweden. Several of the production managers, and more of the organisation charts, depicted purchasing as part of the production department, with the *inköpschef* (chief buyer) reporting to a higher production manager. This is arguably not an ideal arrangement, although it does make for an advantageous flow of components into the manufacturing area and is thus good for final delivery performance.

An interesting arrangement in the organisation of the purchasing function came up in one of the interviews, this arrangement being an attempt to combine the virtues of both centralisation *and* decentralisation. The company concerned had four separate works in Sweden, with the purchasing operation being centralised in the sense that head office dealt with suppliers and concluded the deals. The company in question required a fairly wide range of smallish components, each in large numbers; in other words it was a paradise for the sharp buyer. The purchasing operation was then decentralised, in that purchashing managers at the several works administered the call-off rates for the various components, dealing directly with the suppliers (by call-off rate is meant the number of any given component taken at fixed or varied time intervals, e.g. 1,000 a week, 6,000 a month, etc., with variations to be notified weekly, or whatever). This element of decentralisation gave flexibility to the individual works and helped them to minimise stockholding costs, while the initial centralised bargaining opened up the field for big-order discounts.

Co-determination and the production manager

The last issue to be discussed in the present context of the production function is really a wider one, and one which will receive more systematic treatment in Chapter 6. It has, however, more effect in production than elsewhere. The issue is that of the co-determination system.

In addition to the institutions of the *företagsnämnd*, the 1976 law, the MBL committee and the right to negotiate, all described in Chapter 6, there is another which approximates to a shop stewards' committee in Britain. In a Swedish factory those employees who are trade union members elect a body to represent them at works level. This body is called a *klubb*, and its chairman, the *klubbordförande*, is something like a convenor in Britain. The function most affected by these co-determination and representative organs is, of course, production, and it may be helpful to trace out some of the results.

First – and this is the most important result – this system slows up decision-making, actually or potentially. For the larger decisions there is always the risk of the MBL committee demanding a central negotiation; this takes time, even if the company can go ahead and do what it wants after the *centrala förhandlingar* has taken place. A variation on this theme is that managers will delay doing things until they have been raised with the appropriate committee.

Second, the usual result of delay is frustration. Most of us, when we want things, want them now, not some time later. Thus the co-determination system implies an element of frustration for Swedish managers; sometimes this will be 'pure frustration', but at other times it will be more than this, in the sense of profit, output or savings lost because of the delay.

Consider the following illustration, which also exemplifies the delayed decision-making referred to as the first point. In this example a production director is responsible for several manufacturing works, most of them in Sweden but some abroad. The company is doing exceptionally well, has a bulging order book, and is currently advertising for new employees in Sweden at just about every grade and level. However the works in Norway is running at under-capacity. Not only would it be easy to transfer to this Norwegian factory some extra work from Sweden, but it would also be easy in terms of the technical logistics, and it would make good business sense. The production director has this as a middle-term goal, but observes 'There's no way I can do this without raising it with the MBL committee at their next meeting and giving them time to get used to the idea.'

Third, this kind of co-determination system raises the opportunity costs of initiative. So far we have spoken of 'decisions' as though they are a necessary, and often unpalatable, response to the pressure of outside events. They often are, but this is not the whole story. There are also cases where things are going well and the individual gets an idea which, if acted on, may make things go even better. But if such initiatives have to ride out (potentially hostile) committee screenings, and thus have a non-operational time constraint imposed on them, then fewer of them will see the light of day.

Fourth, a practical point which was raised by both production and personnel managers is that workers' representatives concern themselves with the appointment of supervisors and managers in the production area. Not only does this mean a bit more consultation, which all takes time; more importantly, it also has an effect on the selection process. Worker-representative participation in selection for those posts will tend to favour 'regular guys' and work against candidates considered too forceful or tough-minded. A number of practical examples were offered in the interviews, and it was clear from them that the least-favoured candidate, from the worker-representatives' point of view, was the one thought likely to implement decisions unpopular with the workers.

As one might expect, there was a certain tendency among Swedish managers to throw up their arms in exasperation at the constraints deriving from the co-determination system, but the tendency does not seem to be evenly distributed. The experience of our study was that what might be called 'aggro-consciousness' was more marked in large companies than in small ones, and was voiced more often by personnel managers than by production managers. It is clearly a variable, not an absolute, fact of industrial life in Sweden.

The next two chapters will relate many of these individual points and illustrations concerning co-determination to a wider understanding of the industrial relations system, and, indeed, to the overall relationship between politics and industry.

6 Industrial relations

Industrial relations in Sweden are commonly associated with reasonableness and compromise. This is not, however, something that is entirely due to the national character; instead, it has had to be achieved. Indeed during the early stages of development there was much bitterness. The strike in Sundsvall in 1879, against which the King despatched troops, was, for instance, the first major industrial conflict in Sweden and it is not forgotten. The Almathea incident in 1908 was a bomb outrage directed at imported English strike-breakers. Each is an example of outside interference; at Sundsvall, for example, absentee ownership had come to the sawmills prepared to cut back wages ruthlessly and, although the strike failed because of lack of organisation and resources, the lesson was not lost. The Swedes have since opted both for more control of ownership and for better organisation of the labour movement.

Nevertheless, during the first two or three decades of the twentieth century there were many conflicts and strikes, as described in Chapter 1. Widerberg's film 'Ådalen 31' is a celebrated depiction of state violence, the one and only time when strikers were shot dead in Sweden, immediately before the inception of sustained Social Democratic government.

History of the labour movement in Sweden

A little to the embarrassment of present-day Swedes, their trades union movement owes something to the Danes; the first attempts at unionisation were helped by the Danish labour movement, which set up a special branch precisely to provide support for their neighbours (Jacobs, 1973, p. 31) and to act as a bridge between Sweden and the mainstream of European political ideas of the time, particularly those in Germany. The SAP, or Socialdemkratiska Arbetarapartiet (Social Democratic Labour Party), was formed in 1889, a decade earlier than even the embryonic beginnings of the British Labour Party. Its origins are Marxist but of the Kautsky variety, relying on radical change through a process of inevitable evolution. Kautsky accepted that Marx had discovered what Engels referred to as the 'law of development of human history' and this became 'scientific socialism', the orthodox doctrine of German Social Democracy. This philosophy required accommodatory explanations for the crises of capitalism and so was 'revisionism' to orthodox Marxists. However, it proved to be well-suited to Sweden and to the first SAP member of the *Riksdag* (Parliament), Hjalmar Branting (who subsequently became the first SAP prime minister).

The founding of the SAP in Sweden also preceded the establishment, in 1898, of an umbrella organisation uniting thirty-two different manual-worker trades unions, the Landsorganisationen i Sverige, or LO for short. Although such developments are inevitably blurred by history, this appears to be substantially the reverse of the equivalent sequence in Britain, where union organisation came before the political party. During the early years trades unions in Sweden were coordinated directly by the SAP.

It is interesting to note that, although there are no formal links since the 'divorce' in 1900, the SAP and the LO regard themselves and are seen as parts of the same movement; for example, the LO supplies the organisation and financial resources for the SAP. More importantly, the two organisations enjoy enormous grass-roots support and participation and have been seen consistently by Swedes as, together, the most influential political force in the land, jointly taking credit for Sweden's outstanding economic success as well as for its achievement of greater social justice. This may be contrasted with public opinion in Britain on the trades union movement and the Labour Party.

It is fair to say, however, that industrial relations in Sweden have evolved with more regulations regarding consultation, both for management and unions alike, than has been the case in Britain. There is, for instance, a peace obligation in Swedish labour law which prohibits industrial action during the life of an agreement (Jacobs, 1973, p. 51). Furthermore, the labour force is more disciplined and managers are more constrained than in Britain, as has been shown in the previous chapter. On the other hand, Fulcher (1976) argues, the dynamics of class conflict are clearer in Sweden due to the avoidance of colonialism and of the two World Wars. Scase (1977) has also argued, as will be described later, that the Swedes' greater awareness of class differences leads them to do more about these differences.

In the 1930s industrial conflict led to the celebrated Saltsjöbaden

Agreement of 1938, of which more in a moment, which has stabilised industrial relations in Sweden ever since. Inflation after the war was a further stimulus for cooperation between employers, government and unions and, after temporary agreement in 1952 and 1956, *centrala förhandlingar* (central negotiations) were accepted as the norm in 1957. These involve the referral of all disputes to a centralised negotiation structure and, combined with the LO's participation in the labour market board network, gives its economists the entrée to work out labour supply and demand. In this way Fulcher (1976, p. 56) considers that the LO's cooperation in stimulating growth has been more fundamental to the maintenance of the system than its originally avowed efforts to moderate inflation. This reflects, it is fair to say, the tendency in Sweden for positive action in the area of industrial relations.

It should not be overlooked that the LO represents manual workers alone and therefore currently represents no more than 60 per cent of the total potential union membership. From the start the LO did not seek to incorporate white-collar workers, although this has subsequently been regarded by many as a mistake. Instead white-collar unions formed their own umbrella organisations, which negotiate separately from the LO; none of these has any formal links with the SAP or any other party. Foremost of these has been the Tjänstemännens Centralorganisation (TCO), formed in 1944 from the amalgamation of two smaller groups in the public and private sectors and currently representing about 30 per cent of the labour force. The others, with much smaller aggregate memberships, are the Sveriges Akademikers Centralorganisation (SACO) for professional employees and the Statstjänstemmänens Riksforbund (SR) for civil servants, two unions which in fact merged in 1974 (Bain and Price, 1980).

On the other side of the fence, the employers' association, Svenska Arbetsgivareföreningen (SAF), was founded in 1902, soon after the LO. As several writers have observed, both organisations needed each other right from the start if Sweden was to embark upon the industrial relations path that it has since followed. The foundation of the SAF followed a three-day strike by some 150,000 workers over parliamentary suffrage. Four years later, after an eight-month strike by some 30,000 metal workers, the LO and the SAF reached an agreement (Jacobs, 1973, p. 35). This was the so-called December compromise of 1906 by which the SAF accepted the LO as negotiators, with a right to organise, and the LO acknowledged the employers' basic right to hire and fire. This agreement has been fundamental to the spirit of compromise in Swedish industrial relations ever since, although it did not immediately produce industrial peace. In 1909 there was a general strike and lockout in which the labour movement came off worse and which destroyed for some time any chance of a working relationship between the two sides (Childs, 1980, p. 7). Undoubtedly the aggression of the SAF, representing the employers, in those early days is to a great extent responsible for the LO's long-standing reputation for realism in its approach to industrial relations and its concomitant skill in the conduct of negotiations.

In 1929 a milestone was passed with the establishment of the Labour Court, a non-political tribunal of last resort to which unions, firms and individuals alike could seek redress (Childs, 1980, p. 19). This took place during the years leading up to the establishment, in 1932, of continuing SAP government and came about under the leadership of Per Albin Hansson and Ernst Wigforss: the first a working-class party-man and the SAP's first prime minister during the long period of SAP government from 1932 to 1976; the second an intellectual and the finance minister, who applied Keynesian-type ideas well before Keynes or the 'new deal' in America.

SAP government was initially realised on the basis of an agreement between the SAP and the Bondeforbundet (Farmers' Party). Though not a coalition, this agreement did guarantee, on the one hand, Keynesian policies for the cities and, on the other, subsidies for agriculture. This was the foundation needed for Sweden to embark upon its programme of social welfare reforms.

The Saltsjöbaden Agreement

Since this establishment of SAP government in Sweden in 1932, undoubtedly the most significant development in industrial relations history has been the Saltsjöbaden Agreement of 1938. Not that what has come since has not been significant or more far reaching, but this agreement, named ironically after a wealthy residential area outside Stockholm, seems to have set the pattern for the distinctively Swedish way of conducting industrial relations within social democratic politics. The expression *Saltsjöbadensanda* (the spirit of Saltsjöbaden) is a standard phrase in Swedish. It is the foundation on which industrial relations have subsequently been built, in that it allows for the unions to exercise their freedom in a way that is compatible with a responsibility towards society. As the LO describes it:

It cannot be emphasised too strongly that the first and foremost problem facing the trades unions in their activities is how to exercise their freedom in a way that is compatible with responsibility towards society. This involves rather more than the simple issue of whether these obligations should be self-imposed or placed upon the unions by the legislature. To accept responsibility voluntarily is to give practical evidence of maturity; to have refused would have been to demonstrate basic inability to manage one's own affairs. (LO, 1972)

The important result of the agreement in Saltsjöbaden, besides the climate of compromise, was that there should be no state interference in wage negotiations. In practical terms ever since, it has resulted in a minimum of strikes and interruptions to Swedish industry and, consequently, no mean contribution to its economic success. The outcome, in addition to the establishment of rules of the game, is described usefully by Johnston as follows:

First, the Social Democratic government made it clear to the unions that they had to behave responsibly, not least when a friendly government was in power. This has been of immense importance subsequently for the way in which LO developed and nursed its priorities. Second, the agreement likewise put pressure on the employers to think broadly about economic and social priorities. They saw this point, and took it. Third, and not least, the agreement was a prime example of what can be termed a 'private social contract', between LO and SAF. (Johnston, 1981, p. 100)

The SAP and the LO clarified their relationship, realistically, in the context of continuing political power. In turn the LO established a negotiating relationship with the SAF by which the latter were made to realise the advantages of social reform in the context of productivity and economic advancement. Recently a well-known industrial leader and former chairman of the SAF, Curt Nicolin, declared that he preferred to deal with a SAP government instead of the centre/right government of the late 1970s since, he maintained, the Social Democrats (SAP) have a better understanding of the rules of the game on the labour market.

The principle of getting the country into a position whereby a better society could be afforded economically may not have been explicitly stated in the Saltsjöbaden Agreement, but the practical effect was that the principle was taken up on all sides. The process has been one of international competitiveness leading to sustained prosperity leading in turn to continually growing scope for welfare benefits supported by taxation. The tax laws allow private firms to retain a large share of their profits for rapid reinvestment, high technology development thus being virtually assured (Childs, 1980).

Union membership

Union membership in Sweden is very high – almost 90 per cent of Swedish workers are organised. The LO alone has one out of every five Swedes as a member, this being equivalent almost to one in every family (Adler-Karlsson, 1967). Swedish unions certainly have a higher density of membership, greater penetration of industrial workers and a greater articulation of class interests than in most other countries (Scase, 1977). Table 6.1 illustrates this by comparing Sweden with several other advanced industrial nations on the basis of union membership as a percentage of total potential membership.

Table 6.1 **Membership as percentage of potential membership (1975)**

Country	%
Australia	54.3
Canada	34.6
Denmark	66.6
Germany (Federal Republic)	37.2
Great Britain	49.2
Norway	60.5
Sweden	87.2
United States of America	25.1

(Bain and Price, 1980, p.170)

When the SAP came to power in 1932 the density of membership was only 38.1 per cent and so the phenomenal growth since then is a strong confirmation of the country's faith in this brand of politics. It continued to grow after 1975 and by 1977 had reached 92.9 per cent (Bain and Price, 1980, p. 143), realistically approaching its full potential. The shortfall is mainly accounted for by the low membership in agriculture, forestry and fishing (33.6 per cent in 1974) and in commerce and distribution (47.3 per cent in 1974; Bain and Price, 1980, p. 146), these sectors having low union membership in most countries, of course. The figure for white-collar workers is 81.1

per cent (1975), compared with 92.3 per cent for manual workers in the same year (Bain and Price, 1980, p. 148).

A corollary of this high level of union membership is the level of people's support for the unions and the nature of their attitudes towards them. Scase (1978) found that 52 per cent of his respondents in Sweden believed that the unions were responsible for improvements in living standards, whereas a comparable figure for Britain was only 6 per cent. There is considerable evidence to support the popular view in Britain that the unions have too much power. It is an attitude that is easily mobilised in times of stress, as the miners' strike of 1984 demonstrated, and over the years a number of researchers have documented their attempts to measure it. As Scase (1977) points out, when Goldthorpe and Lockwood carried out their extensive study in Luton they found that even 41 per cent of manual workers appeared to hold this view, whilst McKenzie and Silver (1968) claimed that 55 per cent of Labour voters in general felt the same way. Further, when Butler and Stokes (1971) investigated attitudes towards strikers they found not only that 61 per cent of respondents from non-union families had little or no sympathy for them but also that the same applied to 45 per cent from union families. By contrast, Dahlström (1954) found that less than 5 per cent of his sample of Swedish manual workers thought that the unions had too much power, whilst 50 per cent unequivocally attributed their high living standard to the efforts of the unions and less than 10 per cent were prepared to give any credit to private enterprise. Similarly, Segerstedt and Lundquist (1955) found that 67 per cent gave the labour movement credit for improvements in the quality of life, while only 8 per cent put it down to general technological progress. There is greater participation in the unions by Swedish workers, and the linking of unions with greater social justice, almost negligible in Britain, is quite apparent. The SAP/LO is seen quite legitimately as a bastion against the power of big business in Sweden, whereas in Britain the equivalent view tends, for most people, to be quite problematic.

A strong contributor to the popular support for the unions in Sweden must be the level of involvement. The LO has long stressed the importance of training for its officers, and this training is heavily geared towards the involvement of all. Part-time and volunteer officials lead study and discussions groups, but it is the level of popular participation that sets the LO apart from union movements elsewhere in the West. The integration is such that the 'wild-cat' shop steward simply does not exist (Jones, 1976, p. 66). Despite this apparent closeness of ranks, the closed shop does not exist in Sweden either, although, on the other hand, no one bats an eyelid if known strike-breakers are investigated before admission to the union. Another feature of Swedish union membership that needs to be mentioned is the make-up of the LO. The number of member unions has been reduced significantly, reflecting changes both in technology and in the structure of the economy. The number of member unions was at its peak in the 1940s, with forty-six unions in membership, but this has been steadily reduced since to twenty-five. Of these, six have a membership exceeding 100,000, a further three have over 50,000 members and the remainder are smaller (Johnston, 1981, p. 101). The most powerful union was traditionally that of the metal workers, representing manufacturing industry, but they have been overtaken by the municipal workers – a familiar story in the advanced industrial nations.

The aggregate number of branches in the LO organisation has also been reduced, from about 8,000 in 1960 to 1,629 in 1979, thus enhancing the administrative efficiency and use of full-time officials. There seems to be no desire to return to more localised branches (Johnston, 1981, p. 103), *centrala förhandlingar* (central negotiations) being a feature of Swedish industrial relations, as will be seen from the next section on bargaining procedures.

Before going on to this, however, it is worth saying both that the SAF (employers) member firms are also organised into industry boards and that collective insurance against loss from industrial conflict is promoted (Jones, 1976).

Bargaining procedures and centrala förhandlingar (central negotiations)

The LO's mode of operating has not changed since 1941 when it came to terms with the SAP on the strategy for economic and social reform in the modern era, following the Saltsjöbaden Agreement (Johnston, 1981, p. 103). Fulcher (1976) describes temporary agreements in 1952 and 1956 leading to *centrala förhandlingar* (central negotiations) being accepted as the norm by 1957. The LO has more power and influence than most union coordinating bodies anywhere and after 1961 it took more power over inter-union disputes, rather than leaving them to arbitration. For example, LO member unions must have the consent of the LO secretariat for strikes of over 3 per cent of members, and executive boards can veto the wishes of members (Hart and Otter, 1976, pp. 105–6). This is all part of *centrala förhandlingar*.

There are exceptions to this policy of centralisation, of course. For example, the 1969–70 steel strike in the far north of Sweden demanded open unionism rather than centralisation (Fulcher, 1976). In fact there were a number of such disputes in the early 1970s, due to the pressures created in the process of restructuring industries, but by 1979 they were down to about two a year, and all the while the central bargaining procedures had gone on year by year (Johnston, 1981, p. 104).

Jacobs describes the highly centralised yet to some extent flexible nature of the process as it has been conducted since the 1940s.

> In Sweden the employers' organisation, SAF, has since the Second World War regularly conducted negotiations leading to a basic outline deal with the two main union centres, LO and TCO, which is in force generally for two years, sometimes for one and exceptionally for three years. The hard bargaining is done by three representatives from each side, with about forty delegates of both employers and unions waiting in the background. Negotiations always begin with a thorough rehearsal of economic conditions at home and abroad. Once the outline has been agreed, negotiation is taken up in each sector to turn it into pay deals industry by industry. If, at that level the individual unions and employers' associations cannot agree, a six-man committee of the central organisations decides for them, though it has not often been necessary to refer negotiations back up to the top in this way. The procedure has been slimmed down to some extent by allowing the outline deal to cover some questions, such as pensions and severance pay, in principle only, leaving it to negotiations at industry level to translate the principles into a substantive agreement. In the majority of cases, there is also a third stage of negotiation, over the implementation of the industry deal in the firm. (Jacobs, 1973, p. 83)

This, then, is the well-oiled machinery of industrial relations in Sweden, where the spirit of compromise instead of conflict comes into its own. On this basis was largely achieved the impressive productivity that, combined with the harnessing of technology, provided the wealth that allowed for the taxation that made possible the reforms and the social welfare provisions. It should furthermore be added that the whole processs has been increasingly conducted in conjunction with government fiscal policy.

On the other hand, moves to bring about more equality in pay – 'solidarity' – an explicit objective of the LO since the 1940s, have not been so successful (Fulcher, 1976). In 1969 a scheme was tried whereby funds would be created to supplement the pay of lower-paid workers. How the money would actually have been distributed, however, was never satisfactorily resolved, and in any case it would have been largely negated by another scheme to preserve differentials in the face of variable 'drift' between agreed levels and what was actually earned by workers during the lifetime of an agreement (Jacobs, 1973, p. 94). Certainly, higher-paid workers tended to resist moves towards equalisation, as the strikes of senior civil servants and military officers, protesting about high taxation and the redistribution of income, give testimony to (Jacobs, 1973; Fulcher, 1976). The white-collar unions, supported by the SAF (employers), feel that differentials should reflect 'skill levels'. The SAF, advocating a decentralised wage structure, but within *centrala förhandlingar*, want increases to be kept within productivity, whereas the LO, whilst accepting that unprofitable industries should not be subsidised and that workers should be transferred, believe that differentials should be according to 'job requirements' (Hart and Otter 1976). The distinctions in terminology are, for the outsider, difficult to interpret and reflect the narrow spectrum of political ideology in practical matters like this in Sweden.

In the 1970s, however, Johnston reports more progress in the direction of pay equalisation, as can be seen from Table 6.2. The differences in pay spread are even less if you take into consideration

Table 6.2 **Pay spread, SAF/LO sector, 1959–78**
(mean deviation of agreements from overall industrial average)

Year	Above average pay	Below average pay	Total spread
1959	+16.7	−12.9	29.6
1961	+16.8	−12.4	29.2
1963	+15.5	−11.4	26.9
1965	+15.3	−10.6	25.9
1968	+13.6	−9.5	23.1
1970	+11.2	−8.8	20.0
1973	+8.3	−7.9	16.2
1974	+7.4	−7.3	14.7
1976	+6.6	−6.5	13.1
1978	+6.0	−6.7	12.7

(Johnston, 1981, p.113–source, LO annual reports)

the highly progressive taxation system in Sweden. The gap between men and women's pay has also narrowed. In 1960 women's clauses were eliminated from collective agreements and, whereas then their pay was on average 70 per cent of that of men, by 1979 it had risen to 91.5 per cent (Johnston, 1981, p. 112). The differences between pay for manual work and for white-collar work is more difficult to assess, a point stressed by the white-collar organisations in their conflicts with the LO.

In Sweden, as elsewhere, the growth of the public and white-collar sectors has provided extra stimulation for the union movement as a whole, but it has not been without its problems. In 1965 government employees were given the right to bargain, and in 1966 the teachers (part of SACO) went on strike, a move which in fact weakened SACO at the expense of LO domination (Fulcher, 1976). In general, the LO and the TCO had conflicts from time to time in the 1950s and 1960s, but they have tended to cooperate more in the period since. SACO and SR, however, not having a significant sector of lower-paid workers with equality interests to pursue, have caused trouble by seeking to protect what they see as the career (i.e. long-term) interests of their, respectively, professional and civil servant members. Complications have also arisen as a result of the activities of a public-sector union conglomerate, the so-called 'gang of four', and of a more formally organised private sector grouping, the PTK. In particular, the SAF has not liked the tendency for the public sector to set the pattern for pay increases, especially when it felt that the private sector would have settled for less.

However, all such problems have tended to be overcome by compromise, and significantly the LO and the PTK have collaborated on the co-determination issue.

Co-determination

It is noticeable that different managers in Sweden often give somewhat different accounts of the co-determination system. This probably reflects the fact that the system was introduced incrementally, so that some companies appear to use the terms and practices of earlier rather than later legislation. A second stumbling block is that the representative or negotiating committees in very large companies are usually tiered, so that one may be told that there is a committee for, say, production workers, another for the whole works, another for all of Company X in Stockholm, and another at national level. A third problem is that coming to terms with Swedish co-determination has a 'tilting at windmills' quality; for anyone used to the West German system, the search in Sweden for *Mitbestimmungsrecht*, for certain things which the workers' representatives have the right and power to decide, is in vain. At the heart of the Swedish system is the right to negotiate, *not* the right to decide; what comes out of this is a matter of tactics, values and 'Swedishness'.

The start of the system was a modest law dating from 1946 which set up a kind of rudimentary works council called a *företagsnämnd*. This early law simply required four meetings a year and specified minimum membership. There was subsequent legislation, culminating in a law passed in 1960 which required companies to provide the *företagsnämnd* with information, although it did not oblige them to negotiate changes. A further law passed in 1966 (effective since 1967) required companies to provide information before intended changes, so that the *företagsnämnd* could comment, though management could still proceed with the change after receiving the comments. This 1966 law also provided for the setting up of a working committee called an *arbetstagarutskott*, though relatively few companies in fact established this body. Another feature of this law was a clause permitting companies not to inform workers' representatives on any issue where disclosure would be 'damaging to the company'.

Jones (1976) describes the example of the Kockums shipyard, now defunct and absorbed into the state-owned Svenska Varv Group, at Malmö, where a works council was set up. Kockums encountered dissatisfaction with piece-work payment arrangements, at a time when they were expanding and moving into the supertanker market. The LO advised them that they should pay attention to broader issues of worker satisfaction, especially since much of the labour force, including foreign immigrants, were new to the heavily industrialised Malmö area. The 1966 LO/SAF agreement had set the working committees or works councils to look for 'increased production and work satisfaction', always a strong feature of such agreements, and to provide insights into 'economic and technical conditions and the results of company activities' (Jones, 1976, p. 109); wage negotiations were not part of the remit. At Kockums the works council comprised seven representatives of the company, seven from the labour union, three from the white-collar union and one from the foremen's union. It met at three-monthly intervals, mainly in company time, and made actual decisions about welfare measures, whilst setting up special project groups to look at particular issues. As well as the works council, and reflecting the Swedes' liking for devolution and for cross-cutting channels of communication, there were department councils, which acted as advisory groups on working conditions, and production committees for specific areas. Kockums' loss of £5.4 million in 1969 was transformed to a pre-tax profit of £13 million in 1973 (Jones, 1976, p. 135), although how much of this was attributable to the activities of the works council and how much to the demand for supertankers, high at that time, could never be conclusively proved.

The LO was naturally rather disappointed by the measures of the 1960s described above. However the post-1966 period saw the student revolts of 1968 and some strikes in Sweden, especially in the largely state-owned LKAB mines in the north, all of which were propitious for further developments in the system. In 1972 a new law provided for workers' representatives on the *styrelse* (board of directors). One or two managers we have talked to expressed the view that this presence of trade union representatives on boards has had a sobering effect and has made board meetings more civil and businesslike. Jones certainly observed that the worker directors seemed 'to be establishing a tenable position without surrendering their tough negotiating position' (Jones, 1976, p. 145).

The next stage – the most important to date – is the well-known *Medbestämmandelågen* (MBL, for short, co-determination law) of 1976. It was passed by the outgoing SAP Government, this fact being significant. At the time of the bill's passage it was hoped and expected that the *Medbestämmandelågen* would be supplemented by a *Medbestämmandeavdal* (MBA), a big general agreement which would amplify and facilitate the implementation of the law. However, because of the change both of government and of political climate, this did not come into being until 1982 and then turned out to be a minor affair dealing with side issues.

The main thrust of the 1976 MBL is that both sides enjoy what is called *förhandlingsrätt* or *förhandlingsskydighet*, the right to negotiate. This right is in association with the employer's obligation to provide information about personnel policies, training, allocations between works and plants, and hiring and firing, as well as about the performance and prospects of the company. This right to negotiate is buttressed by what is called the *editionsplikt*, the right of access to relevant papers and documents, while at the same time the company is protected by the *tynadsplikt*, the duty to respect confidentiality.

The trade union side is strengthened in two further ways. Firstly, in the event of any disagreement between the two sides as to how an agreement or piece of legislation should be interpreted, the trade unions enjoy *fackligttalkningsföretrade*; that is to say, their inter-pretation will stand until the point at issue has been the subject of legal classification. Secondly, the law asserts the general *streikrätt* (right to strike). This is a significant provision. There is generally a collective agreement not to strike over wages, which will be reg-ulated by a higher-level agreement, the *centrala förhandlingar* already described in the previous section on bargaining procedures.

The procedure in practice is this. A company is obliged to notify the MBL committee of any intended changes. If the committee does not object, there is no problem. If, however, the MBL committee dislikes the proposed change it will demand negotiation. If the negotiation does not produce an agreement the trade union may demand *centrala förhandlingar* (central negotiations), with the local union represented by the LO and the employer by the SAF. If the issue still cannot be resolved the employer can still go ahead, having satisfied the procedural requirements.

So, on the face of it, it may look as though the 1976 MBL does not amount to much; indeed, there is a trade union joke to the effect that 'the employer has to blow the horn twice before he can run over the union'! This, however, is too simple a view. The procedures, and especially the *centrala förhandlingar*, take time. Thus, at the very least, companies have lost the ability to make and implement deci-sions as and when they want to. Unpopular or disputed decisions can always be delayed, as we showed with a production related example in Chapter 5. Furthermore, these arrangements provide the trade union side with certain tactical advantages; for example, it would be possible to impose sanctions on a company by demanding negotia-tions on everything and forcing all issues to *centrala förhandlingar*. There is also an MBL provision giving the right to veto the decisions of employers who bring in external labour or sub-contractors, the purpose of this provision being to dissuade a company from dealing with any other company which might be regarded as a 'bad em-ployer'. However, whatever the intention, this provision could also be used tactically by a union to put pressure on an employer.

However, more important than these tactical considerations is the Swedish context in which these procedures occur. The right to negotiate enshrined in the 1976 MBL is a much greater and more meaningful concession in Sweden than it would be in Britain. Swedes like negotiation; they dislike clash and confrontation. In Sweden no one ever gives way; instead they compromise. Compromise is a rational and attractive course of action, the operational expression of Swedish reasonableness and moderation.

Piece rates and premium payments

A word or two needs to be inserted here about piece rates and their emergence as an issue in Swedish industrial relations. During the 1950s and 1960s 60 per cent of all work in manufacturing industry was paid for by piece rates (Lindbeck, 1975). This became increasingly unpopular with workers, who perceived great inequalities in earning potentials between different jobs. Yet the unions, in their collaborative role in government, were committed to continuous increases in productivity in order to sustain Sweden's economic progress on which the broad standard of living was based. The result was, as usual in Sweden, a compromise. The concept of premium payments was evolved whereby not more than 30 per cent of pay, and more normally 15 per cent, would be on the basis of results, this usually being arranged on the basis of groups of between five and 200 people.

Additionally, alongside the small working groups, as pioneered at Volvo, Saab, Kockums shipyard, etc., 'development groups', set up by the works council or by agreement between unions and management, are given the task of evolving a 'fair' payment system. 'Levels' of pay are set according to length of employment. Level 1 is for the first six months of employment and the completion of a training programme, mandatory for participative small-group working. Level 2 involves an increase of 5 per cent in basic pay and entails eighteen months with the firm or, alternatively, four and a half years' similar experience, plus completion of part two of the training scheme for group working which thus enables the individual to undertake 50 per cent of the group tasks. Level 3 involves an increase in pay of 7 per cent and takes the worker up to five years since joining the company. Level 4 carries an increase of 11.5 per cent in pay and further training for 70 per cent of group tasks. Throughout levels 2, 3 and 4 there are possibilities for personal increments, which at level 4 can add another 12.5 per cent (Jones, 1976, pp. 139–40).

Löntagarfonder (**wage-earner funds**)

Despite what was described in the previous section, automatic wage rises have become so prevalent in Sweden that, to some observers, the unions seem in practice to have virtually been put out of business as negotiators. The corollary of this is that they have been able to turn their attention to other areas, in particular to the re-structuring of the ownership and control of Swedish industry. The idea of the *löntagarfonder* (wage-earner funds), sometimes referred to as the Meidner plan after Rudolf Meidner, a leading LO planner, is that a proportion of wage rises should be retained and, supplemented by a levy on company profits, put into a series of funds. This reflects the fact that the plan was to some extent a response to excess profits made by companies in the early 1970s – in Sweden referred to as *övervinster*. In response to these profits, wage increases of around 45 per cent occurred in the years 1973–5 (Childs, 1980). The great fear with these excessive profits was that they would not be invested in Swedish industry; rather, they would be invested abroad, or used to buy diamonds, Persian carpets, etc. It is another facet of the particularly Swedish form of nationalism that this is frowned upon so much, rather in the same way that Ingemar Bergman and Björn Borg's tax avoidance attracted so much criticism in Sweden, whilst Abba, the successful Swedish pop-group, were applauded for not only paying all their taxes but also for investing earnings in Swedish industry. The wage-earner funds were supposed to ensure that profits are used for productive investment in Swedish firms.

Democracy has a high priority in Sweden, and it is considered that it has not yet been achieved in the realm of work (Tomasson, 1970, p. 287). The argument for restructuring the ownership and control of Swedish industry is to attain this 'economic democracy' – this is the expression used by the SAP. The funds are to be invested in industry and are genuinely regarded as potentially important and much needed extra sources of industrial capital. There is already the precedent of the investment funds, a levy on profits earmarked for investment during periods of down-turn in the economy, and of the investment of the state pension fund in industry, particularly in new technology. However, the wage-earner funds are also to be a means by which the ownership of industry is gradually taken into public hands, with majority ownership occurring in the not too distant future. The plan arose, as with co-determination, at the LO's 1971 Congress, but in contrast with that issue, at the time of the 1976 general election it was only a minor election issue. Even though the centre/right parties tried to raise the issue all through the elections, and to discredit the proposal, the SAP carefully avoided taking up the issue. This may appear surprising for such a sweeping proposal, but it is typical of the Swedish Social Democrats' preference for relatively slow, careful, planned change and reform. With the defeat of the SAP in the elections the issue disappeared temporarily, only to emerge again as a more important issue in the 1979 elections, although even then the election was contested mainly on the basis of the nuclear power debate. From a British point of view it seems amazing that such a fundamental proposal for the restructuring of industry could remain relatively in the background.

The funds in fact did not become a burning issue until the 1982 election, which actually brought the SAP back into power. 'It is now that you can stop the funds' ran the electoral slogan of the Moderata Samlingspartiet (the Moderate Party, formerly the Conservatives), the most right-wing of prime minister Fälldin's three coalition parties which had held power in the interim. However the Swedish electorate still preferred the SAP at this election.

At the time it was not even clear who would control the funds; whether it would be the LO, the government or some new organisation. Looking at it from an outsider's point of view, there was, however, a potential model in the form of the state pension fund. This is in itself the largest existing source of finance and, as already mentioned, has been actively buying into stocks and shares and building state factories, especially for new technology industries. It is, in fact, controlled by a commission consisting of five trades union representatives, two from private companies and two from local authorities, with a chairman and vice-chairman appointed by the government, in the familiar Swedish pattern of devolved administration.

The strong feeling that emerged at the time of the election appeared to subside immediately afterwards. Most people seemed confident that a suitable Swedish compromise could be arrived at. The arguments arose again, however, when the next stage of legislation came to be passed towards the end of 1983; there was an outcry from the business sector, warning of the dangers of, in their terms, such extreme socialism. One response was for prime minister Palme to appear on television in an open debate; characteristically he handled it very calmly and effectively. At the time of writing the issue is still a 'hot potato' in the political debate; the centre/right parties have promised to abolish the funds if they win the next election, and there have also been some demonstrations against the funds by people working in private enterprise.

The quality of life

Having considered the development of industrial relations in Sweden and some of the major issues that have arisen as part of that development, we can now turn our attention to the labour force itself, with particular reference to the occupational structure. In this way we can examine, to some extent, the effect such reforms have on the people of an industrial nation. Has this unique pattern, for instance, brought about changes in people's relationship to the work process?

Scase (1977), in his comparison of Britain and Sweden, suggests that, despite the reputation for progressive change, the Swedish occupational structure has not altered significantly. In fact it has changed no more than the British occupational structure over a similar period. Scase's comparison is based upon inequalities of opportunity, of access to preferred occupations, of economic conditions resulting therefrom, and of power through affiliation to political parties and trades unions. Most importantly he considers that differences between manual and non-manual workers and between élites and the rest have not changed very much. This he attributes to the fact that the price of labour in Sweden, at its various levels, is still 'overwhelmingly determined by the forces of capital accumulation' (Scase, 1977, p. 162). It is interesting, however, that he goes on to say that it is difficult to envisage change without more government control over the ownership and control of industry. Since he made these observations, the possibility of such change appears to have come closer to realisation.

Some of Scase's points are hard to accept. Areas which he neglects – and in fairness he does not claim to have covered them – are changes in the quality of life which affect individuals outside that part of their life which is dominated by work. These changes nevertheless have affected the relative fortunes of Swedish people. Firstly, there are the changes in the Swedish tax system, which he does not seem to have taken adequately into consideration. These have brought about significant modifications in the distribution of wealth which, even if they do not change all the manifestations of class differences, certainly affect the quality of life. Secondly, and similarly, the gains of such groups as the retired, the long-term ill, the unemployed, one-parent families, orphans, the handicapped, etc., are the direct result of LO/SAP political policies and they are surely redistributive in effect. It has already been stressed how the majority of Swedish people associate Sweden's outstanding rise, from a backward country to the top of the standard-of-living league, with the many years of SAP government. As such they feel that the extensive welfare benefits have been earned and that they are something that Sweden can now afford. Even measures which have ensured that it is easier to change jobs or to take leave of absence from work for various reasons such as child-care (for men as well as women, as we have seen) are factors which constitute improvements in the quality of working life. It is the acceptance of genuine reformist politics, and the linking of social progress with trades union bargaining power, that set Sweden apart from countries like Britain.

Another dimension to this is the way that Swedish working-class institutions span a greater diversity of social activities in Sweden than they do in Britain or in most other countries (Scase, 1977, p. 70). The ABF (Arbetarnas Bildingsförbund) is the Swedish equivalent of the Workers' Educational Association, except that it is much more extensive in its activities; it is also an integral part of the LO and works to publicise and involve people in its activities, thus helping to clarify for people the position of the labour movement and its relationship to themselves. There is also the KF (Kooperativa Förbundet), the Swedish cooperative movement. This has grown enormously, and when it needed extra capital for expansion it took it not from the private money market but from pension and union funds; thus, whereas the cooperative movement in Britain lost all but the wholesale and retail sections to private ownership, the Swedish movement has remained intact. An early triumph for the Swedish movement was the breaking of an electric light bulb cartel, which brought lower prices not just to Sweden but to the whole of Europe. KF also bought a department store in Stockholm, Pub, and now a subsidiary organisation, Domus, runs supermarkets and stores throughout Sweden, all with a working relationship with the government consumer organisation; these account for 18 per cent of all consumer goods sales in Sweden. In addition KF is said to have 12 per cent of the world market for cash registers, and it manufacturers motor tyres and exports them to other cooperatives. Understandably half the population of Sweden are members of KF (Childs, 1980, p. 20). The OK petrol stations, the Folksam insurance group, the HSB cooperative housing group, which accounts for no less than two-thirds of new housing, the Reso travel organisation, and many others, are all also closely associated with the labour movement and the SAP; they are said to be owned by the working class movement, which means in effect the Party or the LO.

Nevertheless, all of this has to be taken in the context of the Swedes, Sweden and Swedish society. For instance, although it cannot be a perfect test, when some American automobile workers were given the opportunity to spend a period at Volvo's showpiece Kalmar car factory described in Chapter 2, they came out of it insisting that they preferred their own working and living conditions. As Childs put it:

The Ford Foundation decided to send six assembly line workers from Detroit to get their reaction to the team operation. They stayed only six weeks, which in a strange country with a strange language may hardly have been long enough to form a judgement. In any event, with one exception the six said they preferred the assembly line at Cadillac to the Swedish system. Partly this had to do with local union independence as against the umbrella of the Labor Organisationen (sic). It may have been a question of individualism as against careful organisation from top to bottom, which says a lot about the United States and Sweden. It is hard for me to imagine an American motor manufacturer innovative or imaginative enough to undertake a Kalmar. (Childs, 1980, p. 38)

Unemployment

Sweden is not, of course, exempt from the economic recession that has assailed the whole world during the 1970s and 1980s. Unemployment *is* a problem, and a very sensitive problem at that. The evolution of Social Democratic Labour politics in Sweden was a process of movement away from pure revolutionary intentions until, by the time it came to power in 1932, a reformist pathway of Keyneslan economics had been embarked upon which tied the party irrevocably to a commitment of full employment. It could not hope to achieve this goal immediately in the shadow of the 1930s economic depression, but from 1932 onwards this commitment became one of the corner-stones of SAP/LO policy. During the early 1930s unemployment in Sweden ran at about 25 per cent; by the end of the decade, by all means possible, including the use of subsidised wages, and of course with the help of an upswing in the economy, it had been reduced to 10 per cent. By the end of the Second World War unemployment was down to 8 per cent, and by the 1950s to 3 per cent, eventually stabilising at 2 per cent.

In the first years of the 1980s unemployment in Sweden was successfully held below 200,000, in a population of 8.3 million. Given the very high incidence of women working – 78.2 per cent of women are in jobs – this yields, at 3 per cent, one of the lowest unemployment rates anywhere in the world at the time of writing. However, even at this level it is taken very seriously. One reason for this is that the unemployment level is articially low; that is, more people in Sweden are on retraining programmes than elsewhere, more have taken early retirement and more are sheltered from the mainstream labour market for reasons of disablement or other disadvantages. For example, there are schemes for handicapped workers which attract government grants of 50–100 per cent of the conversion costs, calculated to a generous maximum per person, which in turn is fixed according to economic progress; for those with no alternative there are sheltered workshops (Jones, 1976).

As already stated, the gains of the labour movement through its political wing have resulted in many welfare advantages which surface in such issues as unemployment. Perhaps it is unfair to claim that the unemployment rate is artificially low, because the control of it is an integral part of the broader programme of reform; Sweden has a Labour Market Board as part of its system of devolved government, on which sit representatives of government, employers and employees, and it operates a firm labour market policy of re-training and labour mobility. The course that unemployment has been allowed to follow in Britain would be unthinkable in Sweden.

Looking at it another way, the proportion of the labour force in Sweden who are members of a trade union is very high. There is an argument that this puts the union movement in a privileged position; however, for all that, the union members will not be able to avoid unemployment in bad times. This in turn puts pressure on the unions; bargaining power depends upon full employment in Sweden, as does the credibility of the SAP.

The widespread readiness among Swedes to link their economic success and its material benefits with the efforts of the labour movement surely makes Swedish industrial relations a worthy subject of interest to the other advanced industrial nations. In particular there must be something for Britons to learn, with their perpetual tendency to cast the unions in the role of economic saboteurs. The British will clearly not give widespread support to anything approaching revolutionary change, yet by comparison with Sweden they appear to have missed out on any consistent process of reform. Scandinavians give the British a great deal of credit for pioneering social welfare measures and, as a result, cannot understand why we continually doubt their rectitude and value, why we continually threaten to demolish them and why we find all kinds of private alternatives instead of putting our full support behind them.

The explanation must lie not only in our 'pendulum-swinging' two-party political system but also in the failure of genuine reformist policies to find favour with the mass of the population. The Swedish unions are not without their critics; there have been strong corporatist tendencies in Sweden since the unions became so outrightly powerful in the late 1970s and 1980s. With the unions influencing more and more aspects of society and policy, it is sometimes alleged that people's support of the unions has to be compulsory; that is, that life is difficult 'outside' the unions. Despite this, the belief is strong and widespread that what Sweden has achieved is to a large extent due to the unions, and this is unlikely to be significantly affected in the foreseeable future.

7 Politics and industry

History

In describing the development of politics in Sweden it will be necessary to repeat some of the history set out in Chapter 1, for Sweden, like most of the northern European countries, has a long tradition of parliamentary representation. In Sweden's case, however, this involves the peasantry, which was never enserfed and mostly held land in its own right under the Crown. By the fifteenth century these rural freeholders were called to the *Riksdag* (parliament) along with the clergy, nobility and townsmen or burghers (Scott, 1977, p. 90). Behind this, nevertheless, is an equally long tradition of royal power and aristocratic control of the offices of state. The nobility and the clergy, notably through the University of Uppsala, almost exclusively monopolised entry into state office, a process comparable with the English one. In Sweden this grasp on state officialdom by the aristocracy lasted until the first two decades of the twentieth century. The first flirtation with parliamentarianism, however, was the 'age of freedom' in the eighteenth century, described in Chapter 1.

The constitution of 1809 was contemporaneous with the sweeping changes that were taking place throughout western society as it industrialised. Sweden's is the oldest written constitution, after America's; Stjernquist (1975) describes it as seeking a middle road (a phrase heard so often in connection with Sweden) between the *Riksdag* of the age of freedom and the absolutism of King Gustav III. The King, however, retained a powerful role, with two votes in the highest executive which, after protracted deliberations by the Constitutional Committee, was to include himself and four secretaries of state, plus a cabinet consisting of the minister of justice, the foreign minister, the court chancellor and six advisory ministers. The *Riksdag* had met to choose a King following military defeat as a French ally and the abdication of Gustav Adolf, but Karl I Johan, formerly

Jean Bernadotte, one of Napoleon's Marshalls, was to assume considerable sovereign power, regarding ministers as his advisers to be chosen and dismissed at will.

The constitution provided for parliamentarianism and the continuing right of the Swedish people to tax themselves via the *Riksdag*, but the aristocracy continued to dominate the state bureaucracy. Significantly, however, in terms of the special character of Swedish government, the constitution laid down the foundations for the provision of public access to the documents of government, right down to those concerning the appointment of government officials and even teachers. It reflected concern about the centralisation of the élite in Sweden and its access to government posts; even if in itself it did not solve the problem, it paved the way for party politics to do so during the early twentieth century. It is, of course, the very reverse of policy in Britain, where almost all government documentation is protected. To repeal the Swedish Constitution would require two Acts of Parliament, with a general election in between – one of the many concrete examples of the Swedes' desire to see government decision-making as consultative and devolved as possible.

The *Riksdag* that was set up according to the constitution was reformed in 1866 – the great reform – when the four estates of nobles, clergy, burghers and peasants met and voted in the new proposals. There were to be two chambers; the Upper House was to be elected by twenty-four provincial councils, whilst the Lower House was to be elected directly, despite the fact that there was still only 7 per cent suffrage. The former was thus guaranteed aristocratic domination whilst the latter was given to the middle class. By 1910 election to the Lower House had been changed to proportional representation, but the élite still dominated until the attainment of universal suffrage in 1918. At the same time the power of the King was removed from the *Riksdag*, such that today he has only ceremonial functions, even though Karl Gustaf remains formally the head of state. Eventually, in 1968, the Upper Chamber was abolished to give the present single-chamber format.

Swedish politics today

As mentioned in the previous chapter, Swedish politics since 1932 have been dominated by the Socialdemokratiska Arbetarepartiet (Social Democratic Labour Party). The opposition is made up of the Moderata Samlingspartiet (Conservatives), the Centerpartiet (Centre Party, formerly the Agrarian or Farmers Party) and the

Folkpartiet (Liberals). There is also the Vänsterpartiet Kommunis-
terna (Communists) who usually support the SAP but who sometimes hold the balance in close votes. There is a bar on entry to the
Riksdag for parties obtaining less than 4 per cent of the total vote in
elections, and this effectively keeps out any proliferation of smaller
parties. The cabinet today consists of the prime minister and twenty
other ministers, eight of whom are without portfolio. There were
five women in the cabinet during the 1982–5 government.

Swedish parliamentary procedures are characterised by a relative
lack of debate in the chamber and by more work in committees or
commissions of enquiry. The latter are heavily relied upon for the
preparation of draft legislation and they come forward with much
more advanced drafts than do the equivalent Royal Commissions in
Britain. This reflects the familiar Swedish liking for consultation and
compromise. The devolution of decision-making is designed to
incorporate broad representation from outside bodies; consequently
in the chamber four-party motions are not unusual and unanimity in
the final decision is the goal. As a result of this there is normally
consensus between the parties in such areas as welfare, education
and, more surprisingly from a British viewpoint, economic policy.

In terms of local government there is the *landsting* (county council) and *kommun* (district council), there being twenty-four county
councils and 284 district councils, eleven or twelve to each county.
All elections take place on the same day, whether to the *Riksdag*,
landsting or *kommun*. The elected members of the county councils
receive 9 per cent of income tax collected to spend, whilst the district
councils collectively receive 15 per cent. There is also a Directorate
of National Planning to coordinate, though not control, local
government planning. This is intended to avoid duplications and
contradictions.

The boards of administration

Just as government is devolved, so is government administration.
The central civil service is tiny by comparison with countries outside
Scandinavia, with only around 100 persons, including clerical staff
to each ministry. The day-to-day handling of specific affairs takes
place in representative and consultative bodies called *styrelsen*
(boards of administration). As an example, since full employment is
so important in Sweden, such things as job re-training and industrial
location, each with financial assistance, are handled by the Labour
Market Board, which, with employer and union participation, in

effect operates an active manpower planning policy. Other examples are, since the 1973 Data Act, the Data Inspection Board, a form of addition to the public access provisions mentioned above, and the Public Control Board, which monitors contracts and agreements in the public interest.

The boards are made up of a chairperson and deputy, who are political appointments, and representatives of employers and both blue-collar and white-collar unions. The Labour Market Board, as mentioned above, is made up as follows:

Director general (political appointment)
Deputy (political appointment)
3 from the employers' association (SAF)
3 from the federation of labour unions (LO)
2 from the salaried unions (TCO)
1 from the professional unions (SACO)
1 representing female workers
1 representing agricultural employees

Other boards in all kinds of specialised fields are made up in a comparable way. They reflect not only the political balance pertaining in Sweden but also other interested parties, as in the case of women and agricultural workers above, all at a practical decision-making level. Additionally, reflecting the importance of local government in Sweden, just as the *Riksdag* has its county and district equivalents – the *landsting* (county councils) and the *kommun* (district councils) – so the *styrelsen* have *länstyrelsen* (county administrative boards) and some, including the Labour Market Board, have district council equivalents too. The make-up of the county and district boards is similar to that of the central ones, but with the addition of representatives of the latter on the former.

The district boards include part-time officials, often as teacher/counsellors, and there is a high renewal rate of members. Some observers say that there is also a high incidence of recurrence (Jones, 1976); that is, that the same few people dominate. In the case of the district labour boards, the personnel are involved directly with the unemployed, although registering as unemployed in Sweden these days involves merely a telephone answering service, leaving the staff to concentrate on the generation of jobs whilst insurance societies administer insurance benefits (Jones, 1976). As mentioned already, the Swedish welfare state has consistently worked on an insurance basis.

Thus it appears at first sight as though Sweden is engulfed in a network of bureaucracies. This has led to people's fears about the nature of Swedish government and to highly critical outbursts, notably Huntsford's (1971) book *The New Totalitarians*. This author, in common with other critics, appears to understate the preference for agreement and compromise in Sweden and to miss the way in which this whole bureaucratic structure has evolved in order to potentiate this through discussion and cross reference.

Having sketched an outline of the workings of Swedish government, it will be helpful to go back and trace in more detail the emergence of Social Democratic Labour politics and the domination of the SAP in order to understand better the special character of the Swedish polity.

The development of Social Democratic Labour politics

As mentioned in the previous chapter, the Socialdemokratiska Arbetarepartiet, SAP, which has dominated Swedish politics in recent times, was founded in 1889. It followed the German model, as indeed did the other Scandinavian equivalents, being dedicated to the inevitable decay of capitalism and the evolution of communism. This German model was Kautsky's version of Marxism, accepting that Marx had discovered what Engels referred to as the 'law of development of human history'. As the orthodox doctrine of Social Democratic politics at the time it became known as 'scientific socialism' but was, of course, 'revisionism' to orthodox Marxists. However, as the first properly organised Marxist party of mass appeal, the German SAP made Germany Marx's personal third-best hope for revolution, after Britain and France. The Swedish SAP was out of the same mould; Branting and Danielsson's programme of 1897 was based on the Danish Erfurt programme, which was itself based on Marx's Gotha programme for Germany.

As well as the beginning of Social Democratic Labour politics in Sweden, the establishment of the SAP in 1889 also marks the beginning of a nationally organised labour movement. In contrast to the sequence of emergence in Britain, where the Labour Party developed out of a mass union movement, it was the SAP which, with a little help from the Danish unions, in 1898 gave birth to the LO (Landsorganisationen I Sverige), the nucleus of manual-worker union organisation. Ever since then they have been regarded as part of the same movement (Martin, 1979, p. 94), although there was a formal 'divorce' in 1900 (Scott, 1977). No formal links now exist between them and they keep separate organisations, but they have worked together with a remarkable degree of consistency. In effect the main organisational and financial resources of the SAP are supplied by the LO, this being especially evident at election times. Probably the most famous of the LO presidents, Arne Geijer, sat as a SAP member in the Upper House of the Swedish Parliament (Tomasson, 1970). There is, therefore, a direct link between the SAP and more than 50 per cent of the labour force. Additionally, the remainder of the labour force – the white-collar and professional workers – is also inevitably affected to a great extent by the polices of the SAP/LO combination.

Working-class support

Broad working-class support for the SAP is decisive; as most observers affirm, the Swedish SAP really is a working-class party with a high and consistent level of support amongst manual workers and lower-level white-collar workers. This is perhaps what the Labour Party in Britain lacks most and what contrasts Sweden with Britain in this respect. Additionally there is no religion-based party to divide the vote, as in Germany and France (Tomasson, 1970). Thus an influential working-class movement represents the interests of employees to a far greater degree in Sweden than in Britain (Scase, 1977, p. 70).

Against this is the suggestion that the SAP has become remote from its membership and that the élite in Sweden now consists of the upper levels of the SAP hierarchy, in conjunction with big business; that is, that the good working relationship established between unions and business, together with the confidence of the business sector in SAP government, has evolved its own pattern of élite formation. However, despite this assertion, the SAP has certainly portrayed itself as a buffer against the power of big business, and the SAP/LO alliance still seems much more of a countervailing force against the power of big business than the Labour Party has ever been in Britain (Scase, 1977).

The emergence of Social Democratic Labour government

The SAP's nineteenth-century Marxist ideology was modified over the first two decades of the twentieth century. More than anything else, the desire to achieve universal suffrage – something not achieved until 1918, despite Sweden's reputation for democracy – caused the SAP to keep Marxism in the background, at a time when, following the Russian revolution, the Conservatives were keen to take advantage of the Bolshevik spectre. The pursuit of suffrage paid off in membership increased by ten times the original figure, after a period of membership decline. The first leader, Hjalmar Branting, allied with the Liberals when necessary in order to achieve socialism 'by degrees', and by 1920 had succeeded, albeit temporarily, in forming the first socialist government in the world by peaceful means.

In the process, setbacks to the party due to the depression after the Great War were overcome, mainly due to the leadership which took over from the pioneering work of Branting – that of Per Albin Hansson and Ernst Wigforss (Martin, 1979, p. 95). At one time one-third to one-half of the labour force were unemployed, and the Conservatives again did not miss the opportunity to exploit concern about the threat of Bolshevism. Scase (1977) sees the desire to change the structure of society surviving through the 1920s but subsequently altering with the progress to permanent government in 1932. Söderpalm (1975, p. 262) interprets this rather differently, saying that during the 1920s the SAP had to content itself with administering bourgeois policies and with working along liberal lines in order to achieve sustained government.

The following is a summary of the SAP's progress to government through the 1920s:

1917 This was the first time the SAP took part in a Swedish government. Hjalmar Branting, the leader of the party, was appointed finance minister in a coalition government under a Liberal prime minister, Nils Eden. However, Branting left the government in 1918.

1920 Branting formed Sweden's first SAP or Socialdemokratiska Arbetarepartiet government. However, the government resigned in the same year.

1921 Branting came back and formed the second SAP government. This time the government lasted for almost two years, until 1923.

1924 Branting formed his and the SAP's third government, which continued, after Branting's death in 1925, with Richard Sandler as prime minister until 1926.

1932 After a period of different Conservative and Liberal governments, Per Albin Hansson formed the SAP's fourth government in 1932. Ernst Wigforss, the architect of Keynesian policies, was finance minister.

In 1936 there was a brief caretaker government, the 'red/green' coalition, with the Bondeförbundet (Agrarian Party) trading on the pressure of agricultural interest groups. Hansson remained as prime minister, but with four Agrarian government ministers.

During the 1930s the SAP expanded the Swedish economy in a way that most western democracies did not initiate until after the Second World War (Lewin, 1975). Given the history of its industry and its dependence on the broadening of the limited home market, it was realised that exports led Sweden's business cycles into the upswing. A 'stabilisation policy' was therefore embarked upon, inaugurated, as were previous policies, by Ernst Wigforss but carried on by other SAP planners, principally Gunnar Myrdal and the so-called 'Stockholm school' of economics. (Incidentally, it is noticeable that it is Myrdal rather than Wigforss who has achieved international recognition for these pioneering developments.) The stabilisation effect was based upon the non-synchronisation of components of the economy (Lindbeck, 1975, p. 58); that is, instead of a number of different influences being allowed to push the economy in unison in a single direction, attempts were made to introduce these influences out of phase in order to produce a more stable effect. Along with this came the consistent policy of 'repressed inflation', thus promoting the first priority of the SAP, full employment.

However, the government's attempts during the 1930s to rationalise credit facilities and investment were not so successful. In this they had to wait until after the Second World War for the series of plans put together by LO economists for their congresses, and the subsequent impact of these upon SAP government planning.

Affluence and the welfare state

By the end of the Second World War the Conservatives and Liberals in Sweden had more or less accepted the SAP's employment policies. Ohlin, the Liberal leader, had even referred to them as 'social liberalism'. But when the SAP took up new economic planning proposals as part of its post-war policy the war-time coalition broke up. Hayek (1944), a notable external observer of the period, referred to these proposals as *The Road to Serfdom*, the title of the book in which he argued, referring to Sweden, that a planned economy was inconsistent with political democracy. As Lewin (1975: pp. 290–1) points out, Hayek's analysis lacks knowledge of Sweden. The SAP's policy has never been a central plan but rather orchestrated contingency measures for the failure of parts of the industrial infrastructure.

It was accepted that the first principle of policy, full employment, would lead to inflation; in turn, in the words of Gösta Rehn, one of the LO's economic planners, excess purchasing power could be 'sterilised' by taxation, by 'investment funds', described below, and, after the late 1950s, by the state pension fund. Mobility of labour should be encouraged to the maximum by an 'active labour market policy' (Lewin, 1975) through the Labour Market Board network. However, any idea of nationalisation failed in the face of opposition from the Conservative, Liberal and Agrarian Parties, the defeat of nationalisation being referred to by the Agrarian Party in the context of the term used above – 'social liberalism' (Lewin, 1975).

Investment funds

The investment funds are a manifestation of the SAP's desire to stabilise private investment in the face of economic fluctuations. It has already been mentioned how this policy was begun during the 1930s as a 'de-synchronisation' of the economy, which was not at the time very successful. During the 1950s the policy re-emerged as a tax on investment expenditure; 6 per cent was collected during the periods 1952–3 and 1955–7 when the economy needed slowing down.

After 1958, however, the funds proper were operated. This took the form of legislating for 40 per cent of pre-tax profits to be placed in special funds, 46 per cent of which were lodged with the central bank. After five years 30 per cent of the funds could be spent on capital projects without authorisation. The main purpose of these funds was that when the economy showed signs of slowing down the funds could be released for investment, still tax-free, thus switching investment from boom to recession. The conditions for release could take three forms. Firstly, there could be a general release period when it was judged that the economy was going into a down-turn. Secondly, releases could be directed into specific areas where needs were perceived. Thirdly, though this was never used, the funds could be directed for specific uses. The whole scheme was run by the Labour Market Board, the instrument of devolved government described earlier in this chapter (Jones, 1976).

Initially, the permitted periods for release were 1958–9, 1962–3, 1967–8 and 1971–2, the results accounting for, on average, 5 per cent of total investment. At the same time, public investment and house-building programmes were operated in unison to beat the cycle; that is, projects were held in readiness until the economy dictated their release (Lindbeck, 1975).

From 1974 onwards the scheme was modified so that extra funds could be collected on higher-level profits (the *övervinster* mentioned in the previous chapter) in order to combat the world recession which was gaining momentum at the time. These extra funds were also intended to contribute to improved working conditions, reflecting a constant priority of the LO as represented on the Labour Market Board.

The fact that profits could be directed in this way, without a revolt on the part of the companies, reflects the developments in Swedish politics discussed here. Consensus politics, combined with the devolution of decision-making through the Labour Market Board, evolved a scheme that was agreed upon during its construction, this being a feature of the Swedish method in the area of politics and industry.

The spectrum of Swedish politics

The broader developments of this period are, apart from anything else, an illustration of the narrowness of the spectrum of Swedish politics. English observers often speak of the Swedish SAP being to the left of the British Labour Party, although the reverse is true, whilst the opposition Agrarian (now Centre), Conservative (now Moderate) and Liberal Parties have together been consistently less right-wing than the British Conservative Party. By the 1960s Sweden had become a proven success and the opposition wanted to risk this with neither an abrupt change of course on their part, nor with more socialism on the part of the SAP. Only on the left fringe was the 'new left' demanding the end of capitalism. The result was more of the same, really rather centrist, politics.

From the end of the Second World War the 'spirit of Saltsjöbaden' (*Saltsjöbadensanda*), exemplifying industrial accord and compromise, was joined by the 'spirit of Harpsund', exemplifying political accord and compromise. What the latter actually refers to is the series of informal meetings of influential businessmen, labour leaders and politicians that developed during this period at the prime minister's residence at Harpsund. It was Tage Erlander who sponsored this trend towards sustained compromise and consensus during his long period as prime minister between 1946, when he took over from Per Albin Hansson who died in office, and 1968. It represents the essence of Swedish politics as they developed during the 'golden age'.

Essentially it has been this belief, that industrial growth and prosperity can be sustained, that has led the SAP to institute broad welfare measures supported by heavy taxation. There is indeed a broader and much deeper range of benefits in Sweden than in other countries, and the burden of paying for them falls heavily upon the middle- and upper-income brackets. It is estimated that the total level of taxation tripled for the average wage-earner over the period – drawn out admittedly – of construction of the Swedish welfare state. Yet there has been widespread conviction – and it has endured – that the nation can afford its ubiquitous welfare measures, that it has earned them. In contrast, the feeling has been avoided, for most Swedes at least, that a strata of idle unproductive people has been produced. To some extent this may be attributable to the consistent avoidance of unemployment on any significant scale, but most Swedes feel that there is something to be had for all from the welfare state. 'Middle-class' Swedes, for instance, know that community money can be used to set up riding-stables for their children, as well as for assistance to the under-privileged. This goes a long way to balancing the feeling throughout society that the welfare state is for all. Another example is the way that nearly all Swedes belong to the state pension scheme rather than to private ones, in the same way that they all participate in state health care and in state education; after all, in a society where to set oneself above others is frowned upon, there is no Harrow or Eton to which the upper class can send their offspring. It is something that is quite difficult to understand from the British point of view, yet it is essential for an explanation of why Swedish industry has gone along with the tide – some would say tidal wave – of state intervention and expenditure.

Right up until 1951 the original SAP-instituted Social Services Commission established reforms in old-age pensions, health insurance, accident and industrial injuries, unemployment insurance against loss of income, etc. At first demand far exceeded supply, and there were extensive welfare queues. However, non-involvement in the Second World War meant that Sweden started at a higher level, economically, after the War by comparison with other countries in Europe. This advantage had the effect of spurring on Swedish industry and so, with growth assured, Sweden emerged into economic and social prosperity.

The virtually unopposed adoption of comprehensive education during the 1960s – another sharp contrast with Britain – is generally accepted as having led to greater social equality. However Scase reports that, prior to that time, there was a greater shift towards a position of economic equality, for instance, between the 1930s and the 1940s, as the figures in Table 7.1 suggest. Yet, as can be seen from the table, much of the Swedish advancement in this respect was catching up with other countries.

Table 7.1 **Distribution of pre-tax income, 1935 and 1948**

		Sweden	Britain
Top 10% take	1935	40%	38%
	1948	30%	33%
Bottom 60% take	1935	23%	33%
	1948	29%	32%

After Scase, 1977, p.55; source *UN Economic Survey of Europe*, 1957

Despite the progressive taxation, class differences have not disappeared, although they are not so significant. Sweden is now undoubtedly more of an 'achievement' society than Britain, which still exhibits clear 'ascriptive' qualities; that is, in Britain there is still the wide feeling that people in prominent positions have got where they are by influence and connections as much as by ability. Another facet to this is that whilst the Swedish income distribution of the 1970s was still, on the face of it, actually less egalitarian than Britain's, it was more than compensated for by taxation. In fact the effective standard of living for higher levels tended to fall during the 1970s; Childs (1980) estimates that the net gap between these levels and manual workers fell from 70 per cent to 27 per cent between 1970 and 1975. This coincides with the period when the equalisation of pay rates was the corner-stone of LO economic policy. This is another reminder of the strong links that exist between the labour movement and the character of Swedish society.

Class differences

It is worth referring to Scase (1977) again in this connection, as he argues that Swedish workers are actually more aware of class differences than their counterparts in Britain. However his point is that this leads them to adopt more realistic attitudes towards inequalities, these attitudes being seen reflected in, say, the reasonableness of Swedish industrial relations, a point stressed in the previous chapter. There is certainly less bloody-minded obstruction within Swedish industrial relations. And this reasonableness is, no doubt, sustained by confidence in a progressive standard of living. In the

1960s in Britain there was considerable interest in the concept of 'embourgeoisement', whereby rising standards of living could affect people's attitudes towards social class. There is perhaps in the Swedish case a hint of this 'embourgeoisement', to the extent at least that the improvement in the quality of life, whilst not removing class differences, renders them less significant. Certainly there appears to be a strong belief in upward mobility in Sweden.

Scase's most significant finding is probably that, overall, Swedish workers are more realistic about the power of élites than British workers, and attribute that power specifically to economic resources, a situation which the SAP consistently claims to be able to do something about. There is thus a direct link between symptoms and remedy, as it were. By contrast British workers are less realistic, tending to connect élites with a 'born to rule' view, which the Labour Party has been less successful in dealing with. According to Scase there is a kind of paradox here, whereby the ideology of egalitarianism involves a greater awareness of and realism about inequalities. British workers have, in the post-war period, operated limited and restricted comparisons which have led them to be complacent about improved standards of living and feelings of affluence. Runciman (1966) developed the idea of 'reference groups' in this connection, whereby British workers tend to use only relatively proximate, rather than society-wide, parameters when assessing their socioeconomic positions as compared with those of others. These proximate parameters do not show up the greater differences and therefore do not demonstrate the need for change. In contrast, the Swedes, adopting a wider perspective, have been far less optimistic and as a consequence more realistic and prepared to seek change.

Progress in Sweden has been at an impressive pace. The nation industrialised late and yet by 1950 had achieved a similar industrial and occupational structure to the other advanced industrial nations. Nevertheless the country is less urbanised than, say, the UK, West Germany or the Netherlands and there is less recognisable working-class culture; most Swedish towns lack any industrial community structure extending back through several generations, and in the present day this has led to attitudes different from those associated with traditional industrial communities, whereby a wholly instrumental attitude to work appears to be the norm. Industry is geographically concentrated and, as in Germany, there has been and continues to be great investment in advanced technology. The form that Sweden's late industrialisation took was undoubtedly influenced, in the first place, by the German model, as were its SAP politics. Amongst other things this has given Sweden a leaning towards technical education, especially at the higher levels; even before the end of the nineteenth century this led to the establishment of technological universities, lacking in Britain until 1966 (a point made in Chapter 1).

Fiscal policy for industry

It is well known that taxation in Sweden is heavy. Income tax makes up approximately two-thirds of all taxation, as opposed to about 58 per cent for OECD countries in general; in addition, there are punishing wealth and gift taxes. However it is important to add that taxation in the industrial sector is structured to allow profit retention for rapid reinvestment. Other funds, too, are purposely directed towards investment in new industries and technology; the investment funds, which form part of the government's 'stabilisation policy' against economic cycles, mentioned earlier in this chapter, are one example, the proposed wage-earner funds (*löntagarfonder*) mentioned in the previous chapter being another. Additionally, there is the state pension fund; Swedish workers use this scheme virtually universally and its funds are invested specifically as capital for industry In fact this form of investment has assumed increased importance, rising from 1 per cent of the credit supply in 1950 to 40 per cent during the 1970s (Lindbeck, 1975). All this has been marvellously effective in keeping Sweden at the forefront of technological development. A country of only 8 million people has retained its own independent motor and aircraft industry, without the government assistance that is associated with such industries in many other countries. Furthermore Sweden is very well to the fore in electronics and telecommunications. When allowance is made for the size of the population, this has to be accepted as a considerable achievement by comparison with other countries.

The ownership of industry

Despite the SAP's avowed goal of real and sustained social reform, the 'boom' years of the 1950s and 1960s headed off any demand for the restructuring of industry in terms of ownership and control. Instead there was further development of the welfare state along familiar lines, such that now Swedish industry still remains 90–95 per cent privately owned. By 1971 the Meidner plan (*löntagarfonder*) had indeed emerged at an LO convention, with the proposal that

20 per cent of profits should be routinely placed in a fund to be administered by the trade unions, so that within fifteen years the unions would thus own and control industry. However at this point the SAP lost control of government, ironically not because of the Meidner plan but over the nuclear power debate.

The coalition government put together by Fälldin in 1976 proved to be only slightly to the right of the SAP and had motivations which were not dissimilar. They did not, for instance, change the welfare structure, unless the solitary act proposing the introduction of a three-day waiting period before the payment of health insurance is due is taken into account, and even this was never actually brought into effect. The reason for their political stance is that their philosophy is in many respects not substantially different from that of the SAP; they share for the most part the belief in the fact that Sweden as a nation has earned and can afford her welfare benefits.

As described in the previous chapter, on regaining power in 1982 the SAP took up the plan to introduce *löntagarfonder* in a much more concrete way, and resistance from business circles and the opposition parties stiffened. The outcome, given Sweden's track record for radical reform, is likely to be a compromise agreed upon by the various interested parties through the effective network of commissions and boards that exist for this purpose. As experience since the Second World War has shown, the fact that the opposition will be unlikely to put in jeopardy Sweden's continuing industrial progress and plentiful investment, which the wage-earner funds can genuinely enhance, will probably be a key factor in this.

Stages of development

The development of Swedish social democracy, as described here, can be summarised in three stages according to Martin (1979). The first stage, from 1929 onwards, involved the SAP and the labour movement accepting the continuation of capitalism and at the same time being faced with unemployment. This resulted in firm expansionist policies being adopted, and in particular demand was stimulated. This contrasted with Britain and Germany at the time and gave the adoption of Keynesian political economy for Sweden its full meaning. Full employment was not achieved at that time, but considerable inroads were nevertheless made into the problem.

The second stage inevitably involved inflation and therefore a 'Phillips curve' type of trade-off, whereby inflation and unemployment were set against each other. When government represents the labour movement as closely as it does in Sweden, more emphasis on full employment is not just possible – it is necessary. The incomes policy was one of compliance, as that between the Labour Party and the TUC in Britain during the 1960s was intended to be. In Sweden broad measures of fiscal policy and moves towards structural changes, with squeezes on profits and reduced public spending when necessary, were involved, all as part of the stabilisation plans described earlier.

The third stage then is the one reached in the 1980s, involving the collectivisation of profits. The emphasis is still on full employment but this goal now calls for structural changes that seriously encroach on the specifically capitalist character of the economy. In Sweden the political conditions exist which make this proposal a distinct possibility, not something that has to be ruled out from the start, although, as has been stressed already, the chances are that a compromise will be the outcome rather than a thorough-going and radical re-structuring of the Swedish productive sector.

Sweden's political leaders

At this point it is perhaps worthwhile to consider the differences between Sweden's current political leaders. The Socialdemokratiska Arbetarepartiet (SAP) is led by Olof Palme. He is an experienced, internationally known and respected politician. Amongst his recent activities has been membership of the Brandt Commission in its endeavours to gain acceptance for a new, international, economic order. This is characteristic of the type of involvement that Swedes would wish for their politicians in world affairs. Palme's background is wealthy, almost aristocratic; yet he has devoted his life to the labour movement and politics. He speaks several languages and so can negotiate with the British, French and Germans in their own languages. He is the consummate master of debate, whether in Parliament, in conference or on the mass media.

This could not contrast more with Thorbjörn Fälldin of the Centerpartiet, who emerged as leader of the Centre/Moderate/Liberal coalition that came to power between 1976 and 1982. Fälldin is a farmer and has none of Palme's cultivation and worldliness. He speaks only Swedish and is slow and cumbersome in debate, and was thus no match for Palme at any of level of debate. Indeed the contrast between the two was so great that Fälldin actually attracted sympathy, something that had to be included as one of his political advantages! He announced his retirement from politics in December

1985 after the Centre Party's disastrous performance in the 1985 elections.

In the run-up to these elections, the Moderata Samlingspartiet (Conservatives), under the leadership of Ulf Adelsohn, emerged as the main challengers to SAP supremacy, accusing them of 'creeping socialism' through the wage-earner funds, government appointment of commercial bank chiefs, extension of state monopolies, attempts to fight inflation through price control and the discouragement of private share ownership. However, Fälldin in his attempts to keep the Centre Party rather than the Conservatives at the forefront of any opposition coalition tended to draw attention to the coalition's inability to work together, as had been the case in 1978. In the event it was the Folkpartiet (Liberal) leader, Bengt Westerberg, who emerged as the main individual challenger to Palme, reputedly to a large extent through his attractiveness to women – who in Sweden make up the largest proportion of the 'floating vote'. Certainly the Liberals' family policy is close to that of the SAP whereas the Conservatives want eventually to abolish public child care institutions.

In the 1985 elections the SAP and Olof Palme retained control by a narrow margin with the help of the Communists. Ulf Adelsohn professed to look forward to 1988, but undoubtedly it was his aggressive brand of conservatism that had driven some voters to the Liberals. In the meantime, the Centre Party appeared to have been eclipsed and the opposition once again showed itself incapable of conclusively challenging the SAP.

The power structure

Where then does the control over major decisions which shape the economy really lie? In Sweden the very contemplation of the Meidner plan suggests that it is really, firmly, embedded in the labour movement, which has made a serious, constitutional proposal to draw the ownership and control of industry into its own ambit. In contrast, in Britain the labour movement continues to press for state ownership, even though experience has shown that nationalisation makes very little difference in effect from pre-existing patterns. Only relatively recently has the British TUC had any kind of policy or proposals for workers' participation, whilst in the USA the interest raised by Lindblom (1977) in 'politics and markets' tends to under-line the widespread belief that government cannot hope to rival the decisive power of the great corporations.

It is impossible to ignore the fact that for most Swedes the world financial crisis is seen as a passing interruption in continuing reform. The debate over the Meidner plan is a debate over the specific question of who should own industry; the broader issue of continuing social reform is taken by Swedes for granted and hardly enters into serious debate. Once again this is something that is difficult to understand from the British standpoint, although such understanding is essential for a substantial appreciation of Swedish politics and their impact on industry. Faced with such far-reaching proposals as suggested above, there is an over-riding belief by Swedes that their system of government is capable of reaching a compromise.

Internationalism and neutralism

Following their determination since 1834 to remain a neutral nation, the Swedes avoided the two World Wars. Additionally, the 1930s depression came late and Sweden recovered rapidly, mainly through exports – a familiar theme in Swedish industrial development. As described in the first two chapters, during the Second World War the German navy's blockade of the Baltic severely curtailed Swedish exports, although at the same time, and with the agreement of the allies it must be added, Sweden's considerable trade with Germany in high-grade iron-ore and ball-bearings was not lost. The momentum, therefore, was never halted and so, since the necessity for a specialised war effort did not arise, Sweden was well placed to resume normal progress after the war.

The Swedes have been very successful at exporting. Consequently they have become dependent upon continuing success in exporting in order to be able to maintain the scale and viability of their entire productive infrastructure. It is easy to see, therefore, the importance of international relations for the government of Sweden. However, given the nature of the Swedish national character as it has developed in recent times, such relations have to involve the reconciling of hard-nosed commercial realism with idealistic humanitarian principles. Additionally, as mentioned in Chapter 1, the Swedes retain a tremendous pride in their own country. In order to understand this combination it has to be accepted that the particular form of nationalism involved is largely a pride in national achievement, which in turn is a combination of economic gains in the form of high living standards and social progress of a more idealistic nature. However, pride in Sweden, whatever its origins, fits in very well with making the most of advantages and, at a more down-to-earth level, with the exploitation of export opportunities.

As Tomasson points out, internationalism is easier amongst the smaller nations; 'a De Gaulle, even a Churchill, would be inconceivable in Sweden, Norway or Switzerland' (Tomasson, 1970, p. 4). Finally, at a more practical level, Sweden has for some time allocated 1 per cent of its GNP on balance of payments to the provision of aid to the Third World (Lindbeck, 1975), a principle that was proposed for all of the advanced industrial nations by the Brandt Commission. What's more, prime minister Olof Palme was one of the more active, as opposed to retired, of the world's statesmen who made up this body.

8 Audit and prospect

This last chapter has two purposes. The first is to offer an assessment of Swedish management, both in terms of the substantive account given in this book and in relation to its social context. The second is to comment on salient features of politics and society in Sweden and to draw up a provisional balance sheet.

The book does not end by engaging in explicit predictions; it is rather that prospects are implicit in our analysis of the past and in our interpretation of the present.

An assessment of Swedish management

Let us begin with a burlesque. In conventional capitalist terms, Swedish management ought to be disadvantaged by its social and political context. It operates in a society which has had primarily socialist administrations since the 1930s, its decision-making is constrained by an extensive co-determination system, and the funds (löntagerfonder) are even bringing the ownership of 'private' industry into question. Taxes are high, income distribution is narrow, management salaries are low by international standards, and fringe benefits are virtually non-existent. Add to this the fact that government in Sweden is strongly interventionist, that the state employment sector is large and growing, and that welfare provisions are costly and a spur to national borrowing on the international market, and the whole scene sounds like a recipe for the demise of profit-making industry.

Yet industrialisation in Sweden has been a national success story. This success is a source of pride, especially as Sweden has one of the highest GNP per capita levels in the western world, usually being placed ahead of the USA (and just behind Switzerland). Explicit comparative studies, such as that by Turnbull and Cunningham (1981), give Swedish industry and Swedish managers high marks for just about everything. So what, in summary, are the strengths of Swedish management? What have they got right? What do they do well?

The Swedish ethic of competence and the Swedes' attachment to acting correctly may appear to be a vague formula, but it is important. It leads to people doing the right things for the right reasons. This does not mean to say that there are not societies devoted to showmanship, status and management by impression; it merely means that Sweden is not one of them.

Again, at the intangible end of the spectrum, the emphasis on *teknik* in Swedish industry is important, as is the consequent concern with the perfection of their products and the improvement of manufacturing methods. The fact that engineers are very well represented among the ranks of Swedish managers, and are well represented within top management, means that there will always be a strong lobby in Swedish companies for design, quality and product innovation and for the advance of manufacturing methods. Part of the *teknik* ethos is, of course, the willingness to invest in plant and production technology. One can easily think of the many British factories where they show you with pride some junk machinery acquired under Lease-Lend in 1941, all the while delighting in their virtuosity at keeping such machinery running. Not so in Sweden.

The fact and record of delivery punctuality is a Swedish strength. Not only do they do it well but they are also *known* to do it well. A country whose industry has the reputation for being able to deliver on time will always score (one need only think of West Germany, where the reputation is so solidly established that all failures are treated as 'exceptions'.) In addition it is probably fair to say that the transformation of business practice in the straitened circumstances of the 1980s has made everybody sharper and put further premiums on reliable delivery.

The strong export orientation exhibited by Swedish management in general is an undoubted strength. However, it is important not to dismiss this by laying out the causes in a way that suggests that no one else (i.e. no other country) can learn from it. Of course Sweden takes exports seriously – with a population of 8¼ million the home market is puny, and even the whole of Scandanavia is nothing to get excited about in market terms. This understandable proclivity is strengthened by a sense of relative geographic isolation. Furthermore, the internationalist and socialist stance of the government is an advantage for Swedish companies in market access terms in the third world. But the effect does not *have* to have these causes. Export mindedness in Sweden is 'all in the mind' (and is therefore free!). Britain could 'think exports' too – it is not a club for countries with small populations.

The egalitarianism that pervades Swedish society pervades Swedish industry as well. It lubricates the co-determination system and facilitates communication. It is one factor in the relative absence of status-mongering among Swedish managers. Associated with this factor are relatively good interdepartmental relations, which in turn have 'knock-on' effects involving good team work, successful implementation of new policies, and of course delivery punctuality. There is a relative absence of politicking, intriguing and manoeuvring among Swedish managers, which is bound to be good news in that it leaves more time for work.

Decision-making may be slow in Swedish companies but there are compensating strengths. If it is slow and participative then it will also be integrative; less people will be alienated, more people will be carried along with the decision. And the obverse of slow decision-making is fast implementation. Swedish reasonableness and the spirit of compromise are a strength. It may sometimes be a mixed blessing, but even if it takes time it saves energy and ensures outcomes. Lastly, the ability of management at the top of Swedish companies must be counted among the strengths enjoyed by Swedish industry. Both who gets there and why they get there are reasons for satisfaction.

But is there a negative side to the equation? In spite of the success of Swedish industry, the answer has to be 'Yes'. To take an obvious and rather tangible consideration, the level of executive remuneration, combined with the taxation system and the absence of fringe benefits, probably has a depressing effect on management motivation. We have argued earlier that there are pluses in this, but the overall effect must be to incline people to do less rather than more. The system, combined with the greater importance accorded to family and leisure values and the higher level of sexual equality also work against a stronger commitment to work, achievement and promotion, especially promotion that involves a geographic move. At the same time, however, it may be that this is compensated for by higher levels of non-material involvement in work.

As well as slow decision-making, there is a certain restriction of managerial initiative as a result of the co-determination system, a restriction that has been illustrated in earlier chapters. This is not to condemn co-determination. The Swedes have gone further than most countries along the road of industrial democracy, and they have made it work. At the same time, it does not always work painlessly, and in conventional management terms there is a price to be paid, primarily in terms of raising the opportunity cost of management initiative.

The Swedish disposition to reasonableness, tolerance and compromise also has a negative aspect, in that some would argue that one can discern forces working against initiative, risk-taking and entrepreneurialism. These forces include not only the taxation system but also the extent of government influence, the norms of corporate solidarity and, perhaps, an undervaluing of individualism.

The judgments offered so far, however, are perhaps too narrowly conceived, so we should therefore look at this achievement in a wider setting.

What has Sweden done well?

It was stressed in Chapter 1 that Sweden's development to modern nationhood came late and that this in fact served it well. However, this has to be taken in the context of the traditions pertaining in Swedish society prior to these developments. The avoidance of the feudal system and the representation given to the freeholding peasants, who were in the majority in the rural areas, must be seen as establishing an early pattern of mass participation. At the same time, of course, the aristocracy never gave up their privileges willingly and even a royal line that was chosen by the *Riksdag* continued to believe in the natural right to rule, regardless of the preferences of the representatives of the masses. This delayed the emergence of real democracy until a substantial working-class political and labour movement had been created by its middle-class leadership. From there, of course, the social democratic labour movement never looked back until the 1970s, the time of a widespread backlash against left-wing politics. Now it remains to be seen whether the SAP can maintain its position when the *löntagarfonder* (wage-earner fund) proposals make their promised inroads into the basic structure of capitalism and, perhaps for many people, begin to threaten the stability of the society; for Sweden, despite its reputation as a socialist country, has emerged as a heavily capitalist country, with nearly 90 per cent of industry under private ownership.

Despite the crisis years during the first two decades of the twentieth century, Sweden had a painless passage to full industrialisation when compared with that of Britain, France or Germany. The Sundsvall strike of 1879, when the King sent troops against the strikers, and the Ådalen incident in 1931, when strikers were shot dead, stand out as exceptions in the Swedish memory and serve as rallying symbols for the labour movement. However, what has taken place since is a model of accord between capital and labour.

As well as avoiding severe altercations during the industrialisation process, Sweden also avoided the more extreme forms of industrial ownership. There were problems with foreign investors; indeed their instrumental approach was behind the wage-cuts that led to the Sundsvall strike which was the first serious industrial dispute that Sweden experienced. Overall, however, the situation that emerged was good, and the relative lack of exploitation contributed to the fact that large, messy urban sprawls were avoided. This meant not only that much suffering that might have taken place was avoided but also that the Swedish character was disrupted to the minimum. As dwellers, historically, of the countryside and forest, the Swedes have been able to maintain these rural links and industrialisation and urbanisation have not engulfed them, as has been the case elsewhere. Of course, the plentiful supply of land (approximately twice that of the United Kingdom) as compared to the size of the population (only 8 million) has a lot to do with this; maintaining these rural links has not been an option available to most nations.

The society produced

Sweden went from a political system based on four estates – nobles, clergy, burghers and peasants – to one representing two classes – labour and capital – in the space of about fifty years. This is quite a rapid change and it did not allow an industrial middle-class to steal a march on the working class in terms of life-style. Visitors to Sweden certainly find it impossible to discern class differences on the basis of appearance. Everyone is well dressed, as any ride on the metro in Stockholm quickly establishes. A story goes that when Marks & Spencer's tried to set up shop in Sweden they failed because the quality was not high enough! Of course this is probably one of those apocryphal stories, but as many observers have pointed out, even the 'winos' on the park benches are pretty well turned out! In order to discover the social background of Swedes you literally have to follow them home, for housing is one of the few social indicators, in that distinctions can be made between different types of flat or house and whether they are owned by the *kommun*, by a housing cooperative or by the occupier, although even here things can be blurred.

More important, however, is the effect that this social homogeneity, derived from the particular pattern of development of the nation, has had when combined with the national character with its history of relative equality. For example, Swedes find it embarrassing to set themselves above others and especially to be seen to be doing this. It is a trait that contrasts very strongly with both the petty class snobbery of the British tradition and the one-upmanship of the American. It is something that impinges very strongly on day-to-day life and enters into such things as labour market negotiations. To the outsider it is something of a mystery how the Swedes manage to work out seemingly wonderful accords in such areas as industrial relations. It must be a considerably helpful factor that the people meeting, face to face, can avoid the war of attrition that goes on when class lines are distinctly drawn in a way that gives rise to instinctive rather than considered reactions, as is the case, say, in the UK. The Swedes' avoidance of setting themselves above others may be interpreted as a failure to assert themselves as individuals, yet if it leads to such successful compromises it may be fairly judged as no bad thing.

Welfare provisions

If you talk to Swedes about the welfare state they invariably cite Britain as the founder of the idea. Yet, understandably, the average Briton tends to perceive the Swedish welfare system as light years ahead of Britain's complex and now creaking provisions. There is a paradox here for, although Swedes do not have the right to such complete benefits, the quality of the benefits is visibly better. This can easily be confirmed by comparing a visit to a general hospital in Britain with a visit to one in Sweden, or by watching someone sign on for the dole. In the latter case the Briton is expected to suffer the stigma of a scruffy reception area with shuffling queues whilst the Swede has merely to cope with a telephone answering service. The difference lies not just in the question of finance but in the question of intent; in the Swedish case, unemployment is seen as the failing neither of the individual nor of a bureaucratic state but rather as that of Swedish society itself. It is this singular capacity of the Swedes, to see people who need state assistance, for what ever reason, not as shirkers and spongers but as potential contributors to the society, temporarily misplaced, that sets their welfare state apart.

In terms of unemployment itself, the Swedish record is enviable. Taking into account all its schemes and projects, the government has kept the level at 3 per cent, only 1 per cent above the pre-recession figure, which gives Sweden just about the shortest dole queue in the western world. Anders Bäckström, a leading economist with the LO, summed up the Swedish attitude when he said in 1985, 'Our whole attitude to unemployment is different to that of other western countries. We really hate it far more than inflation.' Unemployment figures that would seem low in Britain would have the makings of a public scandal in Sweden. And there is a double advantage here; although a vast amount of money – approximately 7 per cent of total government spending or 3.3 per cent of GNP in 1985 – is devoted to labour market expenditure, Sweden spends 80 per cent of this positively on strategy, which contributes in some way to the industrial infrastructure, and only 20 per cent negatively on unemployment benefit.

Sexual equality

Since the early 1970s there has been a rash of legislation in Sweden aimed at really doing something about sexual equality. In this respect there is displayed much determination, not just to make declarations but to get down to the nuts and bolts of the issue. Perhaps the most notable example is *pappaledighet* – the right of the father as well as of the mother to take leave of absence from work to take care of children. This right is actually on the statute book, even if the exercise of the right is circumscribed in practice. Furthermore, this right is coupled with jobs being compulsorily kept open for six or nine months during pregnancy. However, the real problem in Sweden, as elsewhere, is to change society when it rather steadfastly declines to keep up with the legislative changes. The above provisions have been made in Sweden and there are many people who are able to take advantage of them to the full, but still there is the feeling of pervasive resistance in many quarters, particularly in industrial firms where the brunt of such changes is borne. Many Swedish organisations, both public and private, are still extremely traditional in their attitudes to these matters, particularly on an informal basis, even in the face of legislation and propaganda. Not that the fault lies exclusively with business organisations; another example is that, despite special funds to attract women students into the technical universities, there has been no improvement in the female to male ratio at all.

From the late 1960s and through most of the 1970s there was in Sweden, as in the rest of the world, a strong trend away from marriage. Women kept their own name and insisted on individual careers. Now everywhere the swing is reported to be in the opposite direction and Sweden is no exception. The difference is that the

Swedish woman is more likely to keep her own name when married, and the marriage itself is unlikely to take place until children come along. A Swedish couple will spend a long time explaining to you why it is desirable to get married for the sake of the children; such an event cannot take place in Sweden without there being a good reason for it, such is the adherence to and preference for rationality.

There is a very high percentage of women working in Sweden – currently 78.2 per cent – although approximately half of these are in part-time jobs. There are ample child-care provisions, which make such work possible, yet there are reports, from working-class and middle-class women alike, that the main burden of domestic chores still falls upon the women, that despite all the good intentions traditional patterns still persist. The feeling is frequently reported that working women have two jobs, one at work and one at home, and that it is the man who devotes the most time to a career.

Sweden has certainly set an example in the field by its determination to clear the way for sexual equality, and there is more support for the feminist movement and more career jobs open to women than in most other countries. The blame for only partial, perhaps minority, success is not Sweden's but is inherent in the workings of an industrial society which separate home and work and which thus create the gender distinctions of today. The lesson from Sweden is that even the most determined reformers in the most enlightened societies cannot easily change ingrained human patterns.

The quality of industrial relations

The pattern of industrial relations in Sweden must be a leading contender for the most enviable aspect of Swedish industry. The ability to find agreement in even the most difficult of situations, before the stoppages occur, is a gift beyond price that the LO and the SAF have continually given to the Swedish economy. It is simply impossible to come anywhere near reconciling this situation with the one that pertains in Britain. The bloody-mindedness and the continual redress to 'trench warfare' behind class lines just does not exist in Sweden.

The historical antecedents are obviously part of the explanation. No working-class culture has developed in Sweden as it has in the Midlands and North of Britain, and the union movement has if anything kept ahead of developments in industry, rather than dragging behind them. LO planners have been instrumental in every piece of innovative legislation concerning the labour market or industrial investment. The reason that the *löntagarfonder* (wage-earner funds) are likely to be realised in some form or other is that the majority of Swedes will see them, foremost, as extra investment for their national industry rather than as a Moscow-inspired plot, which would undoubtedly be the reaction in Britain. The ability to link a solid labour movement with economic prosperity is probably the single most important lesson to be learned from Sweden, in an era when capitalism is regularly called into question and yet socialism is perceived to contain so many pitfalls.

The *entente* between the LO and the SAF

Agreement between the LO and the SAF is based on the same classlessness and belief in progress that has been described above. When the two organisations meet at the various levels of the centralised negotiating structure, it is very difficult for the outsider to tell who is on which side. In 1985, when the 5 per cent norm for wage-increases was hailed in some quarters as a record low, Stig Malm, the chairman of the LO responded to the criticism by declaring that the low target actually made a real increase in wages possible for the first time in several years. To British ears this sounds like a Conservative demand rather than a union assertion. But, as the preceding chapters have tried to show, the LO economists have taken a leading part in the preparation of plans for the Swedish economy. This has been made possible by the continuity of SAP government (with the exception of the 1976 to 1982 period) and the devolved system of government administration that has been adopted in Sweden. The LO is represented on bodies with genuine decision-making potential, such as the Labour Market Board which, at its most centralised level, deals with such things as industrial location and pockets of high unemployment and, at its most peripheral level, with individual cases of unemployment and actual cases of employment potential. The LO unions involve themselves in cases of industrial decline not merely in order to resist forlornly but so that they can wring out the best deal for their members and take an active part in the restructuring of the industry, as has been the case in the shipbuilding industry illustrated by the example of the Uddevalla yard in south-western Sweden in 1985. Contrast this with the 1984–5 miners' strike in Britain, over the same kind of issue, and the intractability of the Coal Board and union alike.

Wonderful though this appears to many observers, the slick processes of negotiation between the LO and the SAF have, in

Sweden as elsewhere, attracted the criticism that they are the internal working of a new élite; that is, that the higher echelons of the labour movement work closely both with the employers and, obviously as it has usually been the SAP, with the government, in a way that detaches them from the grass roots. It has been claimed that the paradoxical result of the SAP-sponsored long-term accord between labour and employers is that the labour movement has become supportive of big business. The argument is thus that Sweden has become the archetypal corporatist state, with all the doubts about totalitarianism that go with it. In fact, despite its ambitious state policy in public consumption and public saving, including extensive redistribution measures and a publicly-owned infrastructure, Sweden is an example neither of state socialism nor of state capitalism but of a decentralised market economy dominated by private enterprise.

In the public sector the distinction between local and national government is functional rather than hierarchical. The central Swedish state coordinates the country with only twelve ministries, each with a total staff of less than 100 persons. If it is corporatist, and the precise definition of this term is certainly not clear, then it is so in a particularly benign way, if only because the order which people discern in Swedish society is seen to be derived from self-discipline rather than from any external imposition. Furthermore, the argument that it is hard to live in Sweden outside the union movement becomes a spurious one when it is considered how free the individual is within the system, particularly when one looks at the benefits that are available the majority of which enable the individual to do something rather than simply being material benefits. Loaded though the Swedes are with material benefits, their true spirit shows through when they break away from them, as they do quite determinedly in the summer.

Linked with this is the fact that some foreigners over-estimate the 'impoverishment of motivation' that is claimed to set in when the state takes over, comparatively speaking, so much of the wealth disposal. A satisfying job, in terms of work that the individual finds interesting, is extremely important to a Swede and is a much stronger motivation than most observers have assumed. This view may well balance the arguments based on competing social values and the nature of the material rewards that were advanced earlier.

In the 1980s it is frequently said that the youth of Sweden is tending to react against their society's well-oiled decision-making processes and to show signs of more right-wing political thinking.

Signs of the 'new right' are not uncommon in the advanced industrial societies today. Nevertheless, although for this and for other reasons the opposition parties in Sweden are seen as a more realistic alternative than they were up to, say, 1970, there are two points to be made. The first is that the centre/right coalition in power from 1976 to 1982 did not create much of a reputation for itself and was very convincingly beaten by the SAP in 1982. The second is that it would be a very brave step indeed, even for a right-wing government, to jeopardise what the Swedish labour movement has achieved over the years – proverbs like 'killing the goose that laid the golden eggs' and 'throwing out the baby with the bath water' instantly come to mind. As a small wealthy nation, Sweden has not, like Switzerland, achieved its progress through banking and finance based largely on its special status as a neutral. Sweden's progress is based quite definitely on industry and technology, and most of the credit for development must fall on the political system and its relationship with industry. As a liberal social-democratic welfare state, vigorously pursuing an inflationary high-employment economic model, it has consistently displayed a remarkable capacity to innovate in technology. At the same time, Sweden has demonstrated that the stabilisation of short-run economic cycles *is* a real possibility and this stands it in good stead, even when the long-run world economic cycle is at a low level. The SAP takes the credit for originating this, as it does for the pay-off, and even those who vote for the opposition parties have to admit these accomplishments.

Internationalism and nationalism

No assessment of Swedish society would be complete without reference to its unique combination of nationalism and internationalism.

In Sweden the visitor will see the Swedish flag flying everywhere, not just on special occasions but all the time. The economic success of the nation and the reputation it has gained for progress combined with concern for the human condition have together engendered an enormous pride in the country, which emerges as a form of nationalism. When Swedes do well internationally, as for example Ingemar Stenmark, Björn Borg and Abba, there is a tremendous pride in the achievement as a Swedish achievement, even though the individuals themselves may be assessed quite frankly and critically. Yet the Swedes are undoubtedly internationalist in their approach to world affairs. Sweden is always amongst the first to honour international initiatives, as was the case with the Brandt Commission's proposals, referred to in earlier chapters. Sweden's championing of third world causes is exceptional, as is its predilection for chastising the 'super-powers'. A communiqué from the US State Department in 1985 referred to prime minister Olof Palme's criticism of American policy in central America as 'one-sided and provocative' and 'unbalanced'. In Stockholm the US Embassy protested to the Swedish foreign ministry in an exchange reminiscent of the Swedish objections to the Vietnam War. Undeterred, Palme was not long afterwards castigating both the USA and the USSR on the subject of the nuclear arms race, referring to 'their serious lack of leadership' and blaming them for 'aggravating world problems instead of solving them'.

Such concerns are not, however, limited to the prime minister. A five-year public opinion survey published in 1985 showed that Swedes are most concerned about the destruction of the environment, about world poverty and about starvation. Reflecting this concern is the fact that, for example, Swedish pharmaceutical companies have developed the concept of a low-cost pharmaceutical plant to suit the needs and resources of third-world countries.

One of Tomasson's (1970) observations of the Swedes is that they 'remain keenly aware that they are a relatively powerless quarter of one per cent of the world, living at the most affluent level in an exceptionally stable and successful society'. This may be so, but they seem determined to use that stability as a base for loud and clear pronouncements to the rest of the world, whilst, in fairness, practising at least some of what they preach.

Bibliography

Abrahamsen, S. (1957), *Sweden's Foreign Policy*, Washington, Brookings.
Adler-Karlsson, G. (1967), *Functional Socialism: A Swedish Theory for Democratic Socialism*, Stockholm, Prisma.
Aberman, S. (1975), 'Swedish social development and emigration' in Koblik S. (ed.) *Sweden's Development from Poverty to Affluence 1750–1970*, Minneapolis, University of Minnesota Press.
Almond, G. and Verba, S. (1965), *The Civic Culture*, Boston, Little, Brown.
Ames, J.W. (1971), *Without Boundaries: Cooperative Sweden Today and Tomorrow*, Manchester, Cooperative Union.
Ander, O.F. (1958), *The Building of Modern Sweden: The Reign of Gustav V, 1907–1950*, Rock Island, Ill., Augustana Book Concern.
Anderman, S.D. (1967a), 'Central wage negotiations in Sweden: recent problems and development', *British Journal of Industrial Relations 5,3*, p.325.
Anderman, S.D. (ed.) (1967b), *Trade Unions and Technological Change* (LO Research Report), London, Allen & Unwin.
Anderson, B. (1962a), 'Opinion influentials and political opinion formation in four Swedish communities', *International Social Science Journal*, 14.
Anderson, B. (1962b), 'Some problems of change in the Swedish electorate', *Acta Sociologica*, 6: 1 & 2.
Anderson, S.V. (1967), *The Nordic Council: a Study of Scandinavian Regionalism*, Seattle University of Washington Press/American–Scandinavian Foundation.
Andersson, I. (1956), *A History of Sweden*, London, Weidenfeld.
Andersson, I. and Weibull, J. (1973), *Swedish History in Brief*, Stockholm, Swedish Institute.
Andrae, C.-G. (1975), 'The Swedish labour movement and the 1917–1918 Revolution', in Koblik.
Andrén, N. (1961) *Modern Swedish Government*, Stockholm, Almquist & Wiksell.
Andrén, N. (1967), *Power Balance and Non-Alignment*, Stockholm, Almquist & Wiksell.
Anton, T.J. (1975), *Governing Greater Stockholm: a Study of Policy Development and System Change*, Berkeley, University of California Press.
Austin, P.B. (1968), *On Being Swedish*, Minneapolis, University of Minnesota Press.
Bachrach, P. (1967), *The Theory of Democratic Elitism*, Boston, Little, Brown.

Bain, G.S., Coates, D. and Ellis, V. (1973), *Social Stratification and Trade Unionism: a Critique*, London, Heinemann.

Bain, G.S. and Price, R. (1980), *Profiles of Union Growth: a Comparative Statistical Portrait of Eight Countries*, Oxford, Blackwell.

Barkin, S. (ed.) (1975), *Worker Militancy and Its Consequences 1965–75*, New York, Praeger.

Barnet, C. (1972), *The Collapse of British Power*, New York, William Morrow.

Beer, E.H. (1975), *Scandinavian Design: Objects of a Life-Style*, New York, American Scandinavian Foundation.

Bergevin, P. (1961), *Adult Education in Sweden*, Bloomington, Ind., Indiana University Monograph Series No. 1.

Bexelius, A. (1966), *The Swedish Institution of Justitie-ombudsman*, Stockholm, Swedish Institute.

Blake, D. (1960), 'Swedish trade unions and the SDP: the formative years', *Scandinavian Economic History Review*, 8.

Boalt, G. and Janson, C. (1953–4), A selected bibliography of the literature on social stratification and social mobility in Sweden', *Current Sociology*, 2.

Board, J. (1970), *The Government and Politics of Sweden*, Boston, Houghton Mifflin.

Bonow, M. (1975), *International Cooperation for Self-Reliance: Some Swedish Experiences*, Stockholm, Swedish Cooperative Movement.

Brown, W. (1982). *Industrial Relations in the Next Decade: Current Trends and Future Possibilities*, University of Warwick, SSRC Industrial Relations Unit.

Burstedt, A. *et al.* (1972), *Social Goals in National Planning: a Critique of Sweden's Long-term Economic Survey*, Stockholm, Prisma.

Business Graduates Association (1977), *Higher Management Education and Production Function*, London.

Butler, D. and Stokes, R. (1971), *Political Change in Britain*, Harmondsworth, Penguin.

Carlson, B. (1969), *Trade Unions in Sweden*, Stockholm, Tiden.

Carlsson. G. (1958), *Social Mobility and Class Structure*, Lund, Gleerup.

Carlsson, S. (1975), 'Sweden in the 1760s', in Koblik 1975.

Castles, F. (1975), 'Swedish social democracy: the conditions of success', *Political Quarterly*, 46, 2, pp. 171–85.

Castles, F. (1978), *The Social Democratic Image of Society*, London, Routledge & Kegan Paul.

Child, J. (1975), *The Industrial Supervisor*, University of Aston, Working Paper Series No. 33.

Childs, M. (1938), *Sweden: The Middle Way*, New Haven, Yale University Press.

Childs, M. (1980), *Sweden: The Middle Way on Trial*, New Haven, Yale University Press.

Cole, M. and Smith, C. (eds) (1938), *Democratic Sweden*, London, Routledge & Kegan Paul.

Commission on Industrial and Economic Concentration (1976), 'Ownership and influence in the economy', in Scase.

Dahl, R.A. (ed.) (1966), *Political Opposition in Western Democracies*, New Haven, Yale University Press.

Dahlström, E. (1954), *Tjanstemannen, Naringslivet och Samhallet* (Management, Unions and Society), Stockholm.

Dahmen, E. (1970), *Entrepreneurial Activity and the Development of Swedish Industry, 1919–1939*, Homewood, Ill. R.D. Irwin.

Ehrmann, H.W. (ed.) (1958), *Interest Groups on Four Continents*, University of Pittsburgh Press.

Elder, N. (1970), *Government in Sweden*, Oxford, Pergamon.

Elder, N., Thomas, A.H. and Arter, D. (1982), *The Consensual Democracies? The Government and Politics of the Scandinavian States*, Oxford, Martin Robertson.

Elvander, N. (1974a), 'Collective bargaining and incomes policy in the Nordic countries', *British Journal of Industrial Relations*, 7, 3, pp. 417–37.

Elvander, N. (1974b), 'In search of new relationships', *Industrial and Labour Relations Review*, 28, 1, pp.60–74.

Erikson, R. (1976), 'Patterns of social mobility', in Scase.

Farrington, B. and Woodmansey, M. (1980), *The Purchashing Function*, British Institute of Management.

Fleisher, F. (1967), *The New Sweden: the Challenge of a Disciplined Democracy*, New York, McKay.

Fleisher, F. (1968), *Folk High Schools in Sweden*, Stockholm, Swedish Institute.

Fleisher, W. (1956), *Sweden: the Welfare State*, New York, John Day.

Fores, M., Lawrence, P.A. and Sorge, A. (1978), 'Germany's front line force', *Management Today, March*,

Forsebäck, L. (1976), *Industrial Relations and Employment in Sweden*, Stockholm, Swedish Institute.

Fritz, M. (1974), *German Steel and Swedish Iron Ore, 1939–1945*, Gothenburg, Institute of Economic History.

Fulcher, J. (1973a), 'Class conflict in Sweden', *Sociology*, 7, 1, pp.49–70.

Fulcher, J. (1973b), 'Discontent in a Swedish shipyard – the Kockums Report', *British Journal of Industrial Relations*, 11, 2, p.248.

Fulcher, J. (1976), 'Class conflict: joint regulation and its decline', in Scase.

Gendell, M. (1963), *Swedish Working Wives: a Study of Determinants and Consequences*, Totowa, NJ Bedminster.

Gerstl, J.E. and Hutton, S.P. (1964), *Engineers: the Anatomy of a Profession*, London, Tavistock.

Gjores, A. (1937), *Cooperation in Sweden*, Manchester, Cooperative Union.

Granath, O. (1975), *Another Light: Swedish Art Since 1945*, Stockholm, Swedish Institute.

Groennings, S. (1970), *Scandinavia in Social Science Literature*, Bloomington, Ind., Indiana University Press.

Gustafson, A. (1961), *A History of Swedish Literature*, Minneapolis, University of Minnesota Press.

Gustafsson, L. (1964), *The Public Dialogue in Sweden: Current Issues of Social, Aesthetic and Moral Debate*, Stockholm, Norstedt & Soner.

Hammarskjold, D. (1964), *Markings*, New York, Knopf.

Hancock, M.D. (1968), *Sweden: a Multi-Party System in Transition?*, Denver, University of Denver.

Hancock, M.D. (1972), *Sweden: The Politics of Post-Industrial Change*, London, Holt, Rinehart & Winston.

Hancock, M.D. and Sjoberg, G. (eds) (1972), *Politics in the Post-Welfare State: Responses to the New Industrialism*, New York, Columbia University Press.

Håstad, E. (1957), *The Parliament of Sweden*, London, Hansard Society.

Härnquist, K. and Bengtsson, J. (1976), 'Educational reforms and educational quality', in Scase.

Hart, H. and Otter, C.V. (1976), 'The determination of wage structures in manufacturing industry', in Scase.

Hayek, F.A. (1944), *The Road to Serfdom*, London, Routledge & Kegan Paul.

Heckscher, E. (1954), *An Economic History of Sweden*, Cambridge, Mass., Harvard University Press.

Heckscher, E.F. *et al.* (1930), *Sweden, Norway, Denmark and Iceland in the World War*, New Haven, Yale University Press.

Heckscher, G. (1959), *The Swedish Constitution 1809–1959*, Stockholm, Swedish Institute.

Heclo, H. (1974), *Modern Social Politics in Britain and Sweden*, New Haven, Yale University Press.

Heilborn, A. (1975), *Travel, Study and Research in Sweden*, Stockholm, L.T.

Hendin, H. (1964), *Suicide and Scandinavia: a Psychoanalytic Study of Culture and Character*, New York, Grune & Stratton.

Herlitz, N. (1939), *Sweden: A Modern Democracy on Ancient Foundations*, Minneapolis, University of Minnesota Press.

Hewins, R. (1950), *Count Folke Bernadotte, His Life and Work*, Minneapolis, Denison.

Himmelstrand, U. and Lindhagen, J. (1976), 'Status rejection, ideological conviction and some other hypotheses about social democratic loyalty in Sweden', in Scase.

Hinshaw, D. (1949), *Sweden: Champion of Peace*, New York, Putnam's.

Höjer, K. (1949), *Social Welfare in Sweden*, Stockholm, Swedish Institute.

Holmback, B. (1968), 'About Sweden 1900–1963: a bibliographical outline', in *Sweden Illustrated*, Stockholm, Sweden Illustrated.

Huntsford, R. (1971), *The New Totalitarians*, London, Allen Lane.

Husen, T. (1959), *Differentiation and Guidance in the Comprehensive School*, Stockholm, Almquist & Wiksell.

Husen, T. (1979), *The School in Question*, Oxford University Press.

Husen, T. and Boalt, G. (1968), *Educational Research and Educational Change: the Case of Sweden*, New York, Wiley.

Hutton, S.P. and Lawrence, P.A. (1978), *Production Managers in Britain and Germany*, Report to the Department of Industry.

Hutton, S.P. and Lawrence, P.A. (1979), *The Work of Production Managers: Case Studies at Manufacturing Companies in West Germany*, Report to the Department of Industry.

Hutton, S.P. and Lawrence, P.A. (1980), *Production Management and Training*, Report to the Science Research Council.

Hutton, S.P. and Lawrence, P.A. (1981), *German Engineers: the Anatomy of a Profession*, Oxford University Press.
Hutton, S.P., Lawrence, P.A. and Smith. J.H. (1977), *The Recruitment, Deployment and Status of the Mechanical Engineer in the German Federal Republic*, Report to the Department of Industry.
Ingham, G.K. (1974), *Strikes and Industrial Conflict*, London, Macmillan.
Jacobs, E. (1973), *European Trade Unionism*, London, Croom Helm.
Jacobsson, L. and Lindbeck, A. (1969), 'Labour market conditions and inflation – Swedish experiences 1955–1967', *Swedish Journal of Economics*, 81, 2, pp.64–103.
Jagerskiold, S. (1971), *Collective Bargaining Rights of State Officials in Sweden*, Ann Arbor, Mich., University of Michigan Press.
Jenkins, D. (1968), *Sweden and the Price of Progress*, New York, Coward-McCann.
Jenkins, D. (1975), *Job Reform in Sweden*, Stockholm, SAF.
Johansson, O. (1967), *The Gross Domestic Product of Sweden and Its Components, 1861–1955*, Stockholm, Almquist & Wiksell.
Johansson, S. (1976b), 'Liberal democratic theory and political processes', in Scase, R. (ed) *Readings in the Swedish Class Structure*, Oxford, Pergamon.
Johnston, T.L. (ed. & trans.) (1961), *Economic Expansion and Cultural Change*, London, Allen & Unwin.
Johnston, T.L. (1962), *Collective Bargaining in Sweden*, London, Allen & Unwin.
Johnston, T.L. (1981), 'Sweden', in Owen-Smith, E. (ed.), *Trade Unions in the Developed Economies*, London, Croom Helm.
Jonoe, H G, (1976), *Planning and Productivity in Sweden*, London, Croom Helm.
Jörberg, L. (1961), *Growth and Fluctuation in Swedish Industry 1869–1912*, Lund, Gleerup.
Jörberg, L. (1970), *The Industrial Revolution in Scandinavia*, London, Fontana.
Jörberg, L. (1975), 'Structural change and economic growth in nineteenth century Sweden', in Koblik.
Kälvesten, A.L. (1965), *The Social Structure of Sweden*, Stockholm, Swedish Institute.
Kastrup, A. (1953), *The Making of Sweden*, New York, American-Swedish News Exchange.
Klingman, D. (1976), *Social Change, Political Change, and Public Policy: Norway and Sweden, 1875–1965*, London, Sage.
Knott, C. (1961), *A Clean Well Lighted Place*, London, Heinemann.
Koblik, S. (1972), *Sweden: the Neutral Victor*, Lund, Laromedelsforlagen.
Koblik, S. (ed.) (1975), *Sweden's Development from Poverty to Affluence 1750–1970*, Minneapolis, University of Minnesota Press.
Kornhauser, A., Dubin, R. and Ross, A.M. (eds) (1954), *Industrial Conflict*, New York, McGraw Hill.
Korpi, W. (1975), 'Poverty, social assistance and social policy in post-war Sweden', *Acta Sociologica*, 18, 2–3, pp.120–41.
Korpi, W. (1976), 'Social policy in Sweden 1945–72', in Scase 1976b.
Korpi, W. (1978), *The Working Class in Welfare Capitalism: Work, Unions and Politics in Sweden*, London, Routledge & Kegan Paul.

Landsorganisationen I Sverige (LO) (1953), *Trade Unions and Full Employment*, Stockholm, LO, (an abbreviated version in English of the report *Fackforeningsrorelsen och den Fulla Sysselsattningen*, presented to the LO Congress in September 1951).

Landsorganisationen I Sverige (LO) (1972), *Industrial Democracy*, Stockholm, LO (English version of the programme adopted at the 1971 Congress of the LO).

Landsorganisationen I Sverige (LO) (1966), *Trades Unions and Technological Change*, London, Allen & Unwin.

Lauwreys, J.A. (ed.) (1958), *Scandinavian Democracy: The Development of Democratic Thought and Institutions in Denmark, Norway and Sweden*, Copenhagen, Danish Institute.

Lawrence, P.A. (1977–8), 'It's the product that counts', *CBI Review*, Winter.

Lawrence, P.A. (1980), *Managers and Management in West Germany*, London, Croom Helm.

Lawrence, P.A. (1981), *Technische Intelligenz und Sociale Theorie*, Munich, Saur.

Lawrence, P.A. (1982a), *Personnel Management in West Germany: Portrait of a Function*, Report to the International Institute of Management and Administration, West Berlin.

Lawrence, P.A. (1982b), *Swedish Management: Context and Character*, Report to the Social Science Research Council, London.

Lawrence, P.A. (1983), 'National culture and business policy', *Journal of General Management*, Spring.

Lewin, L. (1974), *The Swedish Electorate*, Stockholm, Almquist & Wiksell.

Lewin, L. (1975), 'The debate on economic planning in Sweden', in Koblik.

Lindahl, E., Dahlgren, E. and Kock, K. (1937), *National Income of Sweden: 1861–1930*, 2 vols, London, King & Son.

Lindbeck, A. (1975), *Swedish Economic Policy*, London, Macmillan.

Lindblom, C.E. (1977), *Politics and Markets*, New York, Basic Books.

Lindestad, H. and Norstedt, J.-P. (1973), *Autonomous Groups and Payment by Results*, Stockholm, SAF.

Lindgren, R.E. (1959), *Norway-Sweden: Union, Disunion and Scandinavian Integration*, Princeton, Princeton University Press.

Lindholm, R. (1972), *The Condemned Piecework*, Stockholm, SAF.

Lindholm, R. (1973), *Advances in Work Organisation*, Stockholm, SAF.

Lindholm, R. (1974), *The New Style Factories*, Stockholm, SAF.

Lindroth, S. (ed.) (1952), *Swedish Men of Science, 1650–1950*, Stockholm, Swedish Institute/Almquist & Wiksell.

Linnér, B. (1967), *Sex and Society in Sweden*, New York, Random House.

Lipset, S.M. (1963), *The First New Nation*, New York, Basic.

Lockyer, K.G. and Jones, S. (1980), 'The function factor', *Management Today*, September.

Lundberg, W.T. (1978), *Consumer-Owned: Sweden's Cooperative Democracy*, Palo Alto, Consumers Cooperative Publishing Association.

Lundgren, H. (1974), *Work Organisation and Payment System*, Stockholm, SAF.

Lundkvist, S. (1975), 'Popular movements and reforms, 1900–1920', in Koblik.

Martin, A. (1979), 'The dynamics of change in a Keynesian political
economy: the Swedish case and its implications', in Crouch, C. (ed),
State and Economy in Contemporary Capitalism, London, Croom
Helm.

McKenzie, R.T. and Silver, A. (1968), *Angels in Marble*, London, Heinemann.

Meidner, R. (1974), *Coordination and Solidarity: an Approach to Wages
Policy*, Stockholm, Prisma.

Meidner, R. (1978), *Employee Investment Funds: An Approach to
Collective Capital Formation*, London, Allen & Unwin.

Meidner, R. and Ohman, B. (1972), *Fifteen Years of Wage Policy*,
Stockholm, LO.

Melrose-Woodman, J. (1978), *Profile of the British Manager*, Management
Survey Report No. 38, British Institute of Management.

Moberg, V, (1972), *A History of the Swedish People: from Pre-History to
the Renaissance*, New York, Pantheon.

Moberg, V. (1973), *A History of the Swedish People: from Renaissance to
Revolution*, New York, Pantheon.

Molin, K. (1975), 'Parliamentary Politics during World War II', in Koblik.

Montgomery, A. (1938), *How Sweden Overcame the Depression 1930–33*,
Stockholm, Bonniers Forlag.

Montgomery, A. (1959), *The Rise of Modern Industry in Sweden*,
Stockholm, Norstedt.

Mouly, J. (1967), 'Wages policy in Sweden', *International Labour Review*,
95.

Myers, C.A. (1951), *Industrial Relations in Sweden*, Cambridge, Mass.,
MIT Press.

Myrdal, A. (1945), *Nation and Family: the Swedish Experiment in
Democratic Family and Population Policy*, London, Routledge & Kegan
Paul.

Myrdal, G. (1960), *Beyond the Welfare State*, London, Duckworth.

Myrdal, G. (1962), *Population: a Problem for Democracy*, Gloucester.
Mass., Peter Smith.

Myrdal, G. (1965), *Challenge to Affluence*, New York, Vintage.

Navarro, N. (1974), *National and Regional Health Planning in Sweden*,
Washington, Government Printing Office.

New, C.C. (1976), *Managing Manufacturing Operations*, Management
Survey Report No. 35, British Institute of Management.

Oakley, S. (1966), *A Short History of Sweden*, New York, Praeger.

Ohlin, B. (1949), *The Problem of Employment Stabilisation*, New York,
Columbia University Press.

Öhman, B. (1980), 'Wage-earner funds. Background, problems and
possibilities – a summary', *Economic and Industrial Democracy*, 1, 3.

Orring, J. (1969), *School in Sweden*, Stockholm, Board of Education.

Paulston, R. (1968), *Educational Change in Sweden: Planning and
Accepting the Comprehensive School Reform*, New York, Teachers'
College Press.

Pers, A.Y. (1963), *The Swedish Press*, Stockholm, Swedish Institute.

Peterson, R.B. (1968), 'The Swedish experience with industrial democracy',
British Journal of Industrial Relations, 6, 2, pp.200–1.

Plath, I. (1948), *The Decorative Arts of Sweden*, New York, Scribner's.

Radice, G. (1978), *The Industrial Democrats: Trade Unions in an Uncertain World*, London Allen & Unwin.

Rehn, G. and Lundberg, E. (1963), 'Employment and welfare: some Swedish issues', *Industrial Relations*, 2, pp.1–14.

Roberts, M. (1973), *Swedish and English Parliamentarianism in the Eighteenth Century*, Belfast, Queen's University of Belfast.

Rose, B. (ed.) (1974), *Electoral Behaviour: A Comparative Handbook*, New York, Free Press.

Rosenthal, A.H. (1967), *The Social Programmes of Sweden: A Search for Security in a Free Society*, Minneapolis, University of Minnesota Press.

Rowat, D. (1965), *The Ombudsman: Citizen's Defender*, London, Allen & Unwin.

Rowntree, B.S. (1941), *Poverty and Progress: a Second Social Survey of York*, London, Longman.

Runciman, W.G. (1966), *Relative Deprivation and Social Justice*, London, Routledge & Kegan Paul.

Rustow, D.A. (1955), *The Politics of Compromise: a Study of Parties and Cabinet Government in Sweden*, Princeton, Princeton University Press.

Samuelsson, K. (1968), *From Great Power to Welfare State: 300 Years of Swedish Social Development*, London, Allen & Unwin.

Samuelsson, K. (1975), 'The philosophy of Swedish welfare policies', in Koblik.

Scase, R. (1974), 'Conceptions of the class structure and political ideology: some observations on attitudes in England and Sweden', in Parkin, F. (ed.), *The Social Analysis of Class Structure*, London, Tavistock.

Scase, R. (1976a), *Industrial Class Structure*, Oxford, Pergamon.

Scase, R. (ed.) (1976b), *Readings in the Swedish Class Structure*, Oxford, Pergamon.

Scase, R. (1977), *Social Democracy in Capitalist Society*, London, Croom Helm.

Scase, R. (1978), 'Social democracy and workers' conceptions of power in England and Sweden', in Giner, S. and Archer, M.S. (eds), *Contemporary Europe: Social Structures and Cultural Patterns*, London, Routledge & Kegan Paul.

Schiller, B. (1975), 'Years of crisis, 1906–1914', in Koblik.

Schitzer, M. (1970), *The Economy of Sweden*, London, Praeger.

Schmidt, F. (1962), *The Law of Labour Relations in Sweden*, Stockholm, Norstedt.

Schmidt, F. (1977), *Law and Industrial Relations in Sweden*, Stockholm, Almquist & Wiksell.

Scobbie, I. (1972), *Sweden*, New York, Praeger.

Scott, F.R. (1977), *Sweden: The Nation's History*, Minneapolis, University of Minnesota Press.

Segerstedt, T. and Lundquist, A. (1955), *Manniskan i Industrisamhallet* (Man in Industrial Society), Stockholm.

Shirer, W.L. (1955), *The Challenge of Scandinavia*, Boston, Mass., Little, Brown.

Sjoberg, G., Hancock, M.D. and White Jnr, O. (1967), *Politics in the Post-Welfare State: A Comparison of the US and Sweden*, Bloomington, Ind., Indiana University.

Smith, E.O. (1981), *Trade Unions in the Developed Economies*, London, Croom Helm.

Söderpalm, S.A. (1975), 'The crisis agreement and the Social Democratic road to power', in Koblik.

Stenholm, B. (1970), *Education in Sweden*, Stockholm, Swedish Institute.

Stjernquist, N. (1975), 'The creation of the 1809 constitution', in Koblik.

Strender, B. (1971), *What Is a Just Wage?*, Stockholm, SAF.

Sundgran, N.P. (1970), *New Swedish Cinema*, Stockholm, Swedish Institute.

Svalastoga, K. and Carlsson, G. (1961), 'Social stratification and social mobility in Scandinavia', *Sociological Inquiry*, 31.

Swedenborg, B. (1974), *Swedish Direct Investment Abroad, 1965–1970*, Stockholm, Almquist & Wiksell.

Swedish Institute of International Affairs (1956), *Sweden and The UN*, New York, Manhattan.

Telesis Inc. (1980), *The Engineering Industry and Swedish Industrial Policy*, Report to the Sveriges Mekanförbund, October.

Thoenes, P. (1966), *The Elite in the Welfare State*, New York, Free Press.

Tilton, T.A. (1979), 'The Swedish road to socialism', *American Political Science Review*, 73, 4, pp.505–20.

Tingsten, H. (1949), *The Debate on the Foreign Policy of Sweden, 1918–1939*, Oxford University Press.

Tingsten, H. (1973), *The Swedish Social Democrats*, Totowa, NJ, Bedminster.

Tomasson, R.F. (1969), 'The extraordinary success of the Swedish Social Democrats', *Journal of Politics*, 31, pp.772–98.

Tomasson, R.F. (1970), *Sweden: Prototype of Modern Society*, New York, Random House.

Turnbull, P.W. and Cunningham, M.T. (eds) (1981), *International Marketing and Purchashing*, London, Macmillan.

Turvey, R. (ed.) (1952), *Wages Policy Under Full Employment*, London, Hodge.

Urquhart, B. (1972), *Hammarskjold*, New York, Knopf.

Verney, D.V. (1957), *Parliamentary Reform in Sweden 1866–1921*, Oxford, Clarendon Press.

Verney, D.V. (1959), *Public Enterprise in Sweden*, Liverpool University Press.

Von Otter, C. (1980), 'Swedish welfare capitalism: the role of the state', in Scase, R. (ed.), *The State in Western Europe*, London, Croom Helm.

Weibull, J. (1968), *Sweden, 1918–1968*, London, University College.

Wiener, M.J. (1981), *English Culture and the Decline of the Industrial Spirit 1850–1980*, Cambridge University Press.

Wheeler, C. (1975), *White-Collar Power, Changing Patterns of Interest Group Behaviour in Sweden*, Urbana, Ill., University of Illinois Press.

Wizelius, I. (ed.) (1967), *Sweden in the Sixties: a Symposium of Facts and Views in 17 Chapters*, Stockholm, Almquist & Wiksell.

Index